The Texas
Cowboy Kitchen

Grady Spears
with June Naylor

Photographs by Erwin E. Smith
from the Amon Carter Museum Collection

Food Photography by Ralph Lauer

Andrews McMeel
Publishing, LLC
Kansas City · Sydney · London

Andrews McMeel Publishing, LLC
an Andrews McMeel Universal company
1130 Walnut Street, Kansas City, Missouri 64106

www.andrewsmcmeel.com

First published in 2003 by Texas Monthly Custom Publishing, 701 Brazos, Suite 1600, Austin, Texas 78701.

11 SDB 10 9 8 7 6 5

ISBN: 978-0-7407-6973-3

Library of Congress Control Number: 2007928068

Food photography: Ralph Lauer
Food and prop styling: Meda Kessler
Portrait styling: Gary Leatherwood
Archival photography: Erwin E. Smith
Archival photos from the Amon Carter Museum Collection, Fort Worth, Texas

The Texas Cowboy Kitchen

For Missy and Janie

Contents

PAGE 2
Some Spur Ranch Cowboys Resting and Working Around the Clock and Hoodlum Wagons, Spur Ranch, Texas. ca. 1910.

THIS SPREAD
The Matador Wagon Cook [Harry Stewart] Making a Cobbler. Matador Ranch, Texas 1908.

I F THERE'S ANYONE WHO UNDERSTANDS great Texas food and appreciates the state's cowboy heritage, it's Grady Spears. You see, I'm right there with him. Baseball was a wonderful career for me, but cattle ranching has always been my primary passion. So it stands to reason that I'd come across somebody like Grady. ✪ Since meeting in 1998, Grady and I have worked together on several projects. He's rustled up some darn good suppers at fund-raisers, including those for the Ranch Management Program at Texas Christian University, in Fort Worth. He's cooked hundreds of steaks at my ranch, and we even appeared together in a special program for the Food TV Network called *The Cowboy's Kitchen*. These events gave me the chance to see that Grady's a true Texas cowboy who knows the importance of making the best in Texas grub. ✪ Grady's probably the only guy I know who could dress up Frito pie and make it pretty, and the only cook who'd think of marinating skirt steak in Dr Pepper for making tostadas. Face it, the only person who would do all that is someone who's as at ease in a worn pair of leather chaps as he is wielding a sauté pan. ✪ I think you'll like *The Texas Cowboy Kitchen* for several reasons. It's packed with the sensational foods of Texas, all improved upon by Grady, who happens to be the nation's leading contemporary cowboy cook. On top of that, it's filled with the lore, legend, and romance of the famous Chisholm Trail and blessed with exceptional pictures by Erwin E. Smith, the foremost cowboy photographer in history. ✪ The book captures an era when chuck-wagon cooks on the cattle drive kept the cowpokes fed with beans, tortillas, beef jerky, and stews. And while cowboys of the Chisholm Trail days didn't have such treasures as beef tenderloin with Hollandaise Diablo or pan-roasted trout ranchero, trail-weary travelers today can find that kind of happiness at Grady's restaurants and in this book. Sure, the ingredients have been around for the past 150 years, but you can bet that nobody has ever put them together in the irresistible fashion that has become synonymous with Grady Spears' renowned cowboy cooking. ✪ It's all here, with much more. Enjoy your reading, your history lessons, and great eating. *Nolan Ryan*

June Naylor and Grady Spears in Fort Worth, Texas.

The Chisholm Trail

WHILE THE CHISHOLM Trail had a far-reaching impact on American life, business, and culture, it proved a critical element in the economic recovery of Texas after the Civil War when the Lone Star State was left in a desperate condition with little currency to rebuild its economy. This trail was the route for hundreds of thousands of Longhorns to travel north to market, thereby creating a strong cattle industry in Texas. Moreover, the Chisholm Trail established the image of the American cowboy as a brave man on horseback, able to cope with a broad range of challenges in the face of the untamed West.

During the years before the Civil War, the Shawnee Trail became an important route for taking cattle to markets in the Midwest. This trail took cattle to Missouri and then northward, but the volume of traffic was not great in comparison to what was to come later. A simple matter of economics caused the Chisholm Trail to come into existence. During the Civil War (1861–1865), Texas ranches were largely abandoned as young men went into military service and existing cattle herds multiplied in the wild. Traditional markets were cut off because of the war, and it was difficult to move the cattle to support the Southern armies fighting many miles away. As a result, Texas became filled with thousands of wild, unbranded Longhorn cattle by the end of the Civil War. However, these cattle were worth little unless they were taken to markets in the large cities of the Midwest or the East. The Chisholm Trail came into existence to connect the large quantities of beef in Texas to supply the pent-up demand that existed throughout the North after the war.

The Chisholm Trail provided flat grasslands to take the herds of cattle on a direct route north to the towns in Kansas with rail lines, then onward to meat-packing houses in the Midwest and East. After the Civil War, Joseph G. McCoy, a businessman from Illinois, identified the opportunity to sell the Texas cattle in Kansas at towns where train service was just becoming available. He promoted the idea to the railroads and to the Texas ranchers, and by 1867, the first cattle were being moved up toward Kansas.

McCoy identified the logical route to take the cattle north. A portion of his proposed route had previously been mapped out and used by a well-known frontiersman by the name of Jesse Chisholm. Chisholm had moved goods and some cattle from central Indian Territory to southern Kansas, and people referred to this as the Chisholm Trail. As cattle began to come up from Texas, the drovers used Jesse Chisholm's route in Indian Territory. Over time, the entire route became commonly known as the Chisholm Trail.

Cattle from across South Texas would be gathered into herds of two thousand or more head for movement north. The trail drivers would take the cattle along a corridor of flat grasslands that runs from south to in central Texas, choosing a path that would offer water along the way. A small group of cowboys numbering only 10 to 12 would handle the cattle for the entire trip north, which could take more than three months. Using this system, cowboys took more than six million cattle "up the trail."

Life on the trail was dangerous, difficult, and dirty. River crossings always had the potential for problems, such as flash floods, quicksand, or snakes. Farmers, Indians, and rustlers were not friendly to the cattle drives as they crossed the 800 miles on the way to the Kansas railhead. The trail drive only passed by a few towns of any size, and these "cowtowns," such as Fort Worth, provided the cowboys the brief opportunity to kick up their heels for a short time. Once the cowboys reached Abilene, Ellsworth, or Dodge City, the end of the trail was a time of excitement and sometimes an opportunity for trouble with local law enforcement. If the cowboy was lucky, he might keep some of his earnings to take back to his Texas home.

Jesse Chisholm

The Chisholm Trail era lasted only from 1867–1884, but the image of the "wild and woolly" cowboy emerged because of the popular dime magazines that were being written about their exploits. Within a few years, a long list of books about the trail drives began to be published, such as Charles Siringo's *A Texas Cowboy* (1885) and J. Marvin Hunter's *Trail Drivers of Texas* (1925.) The Chisholm Trail also became the subject for many movies. Two of the best are *Red River* and *Lonesome Dove*. The TV series *Rawhide* also focused on the trail drive. As a result of this considerable media attention, the cowboy became an important American icon. The Chisholm Trail played a key role in this development by creating the landscape, setting, and era in which the cowboy demonstrated courage, determination, and strength.

Today's visitors to Texas can obtain a copy of the Texas Historical Commission's brochure "The Chisholm Trail: Exploring the Folklore and Legacy," published in 2002. The up-to-date guide details several places to visit along the Chisholm Trail in Texas, from far South Texas along the Rio Grande northward about 600 miles to the Red River. In South Texas, Kingsville is home to the famous King Ranch, a region that produced hundreds of thousands of cattle during the Trail era. The Interstate 35 corridor generally follows the original Chisholm Trail, and there are many historic communities with trail drive heritage along the way including Yoakum, Lockhart, Round Rock, Georgetown, Salado, and Belton. West of Waco, the route can be followed along some interesting state roads through Clifton, Meridian, and Cleburne. Fort Worth, long known as "Cowtown," is home to the famous Chisholm Trail mural in downtown, the Sid Richardson Collection of Western Art, the Cattle Raisers Museum, the Texas Cowboy Hall of Fame, the Amon Carter Museum, the National Cowgirl Museum, the Stockyards National Historic District, and you can even experience the Fort Worth Herd—a daily cattle drive.

Jack Potter's Map of Cattle Trails (1935) shows cattle trails as used from 1866 to 1895 to northern markets. Prepared by A. C. Loveless, Clayton, New Mexico. Courtesy of the Center for American History, UT-Austin.

From Fort Worth, the trail traveled north through Bowie and Nocona to the Red River. The route through Oklahoma and Kansas offers interest, as well, particularly at the Chisholm Trail Museum in Duncan, Oklahoma. Through these excellent historic sites, you can experience one of the most famous cattle trails in American history.

More Chisholm Trail and related period history can be found in such books as *The Chisholm Trail*, by Wayne Gard (University of Oklahoma Press), *The Longhorns*, by J. Frank Dobie (Bramhall Press), *Cow People*, by J. Frank Dobie (University of Texas Press), *The Chisholm Trail in American History*, by William R. Sanford (Enslow Publishers), and *Trail Drivers of Texas: Interesting Sketches of Early Cowboys and Their Experiences on the Range and on the Trail During the Days That Tried Men*, by J. Marvin Hunter (University of Texas Press).

Douglas Harman, Retired
President & CEO, Fort Worth Convention & Visitors Bureau

Cowboy Photographer

*Erwin E. Smith and His Mount
Overlooking the Country from a High
Point on the JA Ranch, Texas. 1908.*

ERWIN E. SMITH (1886–1947) always wanted to be a cowboy and an artist. Growing up in Bonham, a small town in North Texas, Smith saw the era of the great trail drives come to an end, and he knew the old ways of the cowboy were fast disappearing. The powerful legend and myth of the cowboy, however, was just beginning. Popular literature, the work of artists like Frederic Remington and Charles M. Russell, and the fledgling film industry promoted a romantic and often inaccurate image of the cowboy. For his part, Smith resolved to capture the cowboy as he really was.

A good artist knows that to portray a subject as accurately as possible requires an understanding of the subject, and Smith took every opportunity to gain experience as a working cowboy. As a youth, he spent summers on his uncle's ranch near Quanah, Texas. The land bordered the Great Western Cattle Trail, where hundreds of thousands of Longhorns were herded north in the 1880s. During those summers, Smith began to acquire the expertise of a trained cowhand.

Working in the West was one thing, but capturing it artistically was an immense challenge—"From the first time I laid eyes on the sun burnt plains of the West, with its grand scenery, I have been in love with its still, enchanted solitude. Its change of colors no artist can portray," he wrote in his journal. He persevered, though, studying sculpture and painting at the Art Institute of Chicago and the School of the Boston Museum of Fine Arts. While not in school, he traveled throughout Texas, New Mexico, and Arizona making photographs of roundups and other ranching scenes to use as studies for his sculptures and paintings. With time, however, he began to realize that these photographs were themselves historical documents and works of art. Before long, his firsthand knowledge of ranching, coupled with his understanding of photographic composition and willingness to experiment with the medium, all coalesced to produce what one contemporary critic called "the finest pictures of range life ever taken."

When Erwin Smith died in 1947, his half-sister, Mary Alice Pettis, preserved his original negatives and prints in a bank vault. She eventually deposited a large number of the negatives with the Library of Congress, but she never abandoned her wish to unite the entire collection in Texas. In 1986 she bequeathed her collection of Smith's work and those on loan at the Library of Congress—a total of more than 2,000 negatives and 700 vintage prints—to the Amon Carter Museum.

The Carter was established through the generosity of Amon G. Carter, Sr. (1879-1955), to house his collection of paintings and sculpture by Remington and Russell. The museum's mission is "to collect, preserve, and exhibit the finest examples of American art, and to serve an educational role through exhibitions, publications, and programs devoted to the study of American art." Since its inception in 1961, the museum has collected nearly a quarter of a million objects and compiled one of the nation's most important collections of American photographs. Smith would have been proud to be represented in this prestigious collection and likewise in this handsome book, which helps to preserve for future generations both the romance and the rugged realities of the cowboy and his life on the open range.

*Barbara McCandless
Curator of Photographic Collections, Amon Carter Museum*

TAKE ONE LOOK AT A TOWN with a bold, unshakable sense of pleasure, and you can bet it's a place that has a certain past—a word we offer with a knowing wink. Fort Worth bursts with that kind of stirring energy: Whereas the more prudish types might blush at this old Texas cattle town's heritage, its more appreciative, lore-loving natives (like us) take a profound, if perhaps brazen, sense of pride in its coarse, untamed, and at times tawdry beginnings. We haven't found another place with a deeper, more romantic Western legacy, nor a place more truly affected by the Chisholm Trail. ✪ Named for Jesse Chisholm, an Indian trader whose wagon wheels carved the original path between the North Canadian River near Wichita, Kansas, and the Arkansas River near Yukon, Oklahoma, the Chisholm Trail soon became the primary cattle drive route that found its southern starting point along the Rio Grande, way down at Texas' tip. The legend of cattle drives was born, as millions of Texas Longhorn were eventually herded through this artery northward to railheads and markets in Kansas. ✪ Although the route through Texas would meander the tiniest bit east and west— it's been noted by more than a few cattle-drive historians that Longhorns were loathe to walk in a straight line—there was at least one unfailing occurrence: This well-trodden cattle trail would cross rivers at the same, exact place on every single drive for some dozen years. Among these abiding sites was the Trinity Ford in Fort Worth, just below the junction of the Clear and West forks of the Trinity River. ✪ Fort Worth was not quite twenty years old when the Chisholm Trail first passed through, but it served immediately as a major, essential trading and supply depot for cattlemen—to say nothing of a welcome time out for cowboys who needed to blow off some steam for a few days after long, back-breaking weeks in the saddle on a tedious, bone-tiring trail. Hot baths and real beds rounded out the fulfillment initiated at saloons, which provided dreamed-of whiskey, card games, and soft, gentle companionship. ✪ The cowpokes almost certainly ate best, too, during their bouts of Fort Worth R'n'R. Although the chuck-wagon cooks who accompanied every drive kept the hands fed with stews, beef jerky, and beans, the cowboys found unmatched gratification in Fort Worth by tearing into platters of freshly battered fried chicken with bowls of gravy and sides of greens and perhaps garden-fresh tomatoes and melons and slices of just-baked peach pie. ✪ Fort Worth remains a place fervently tethered to its cowboy past and its Chisholm Trail heritage, as witnessed by the city's official Longhorn herd and a local fondness for the nickname "Cowtown." And perhaps as significantly, it's the favorite stop in Texas for sensational cowboy grub—the stylish sort, of course, treasured at Grady's restaurants. ✪ Within these pages you'll be tempted by such appetizers as tamales stuffed with barbecue quail and topped with avocado cream and Frito pie with venison chili and Texas pico; side dishes such as mashed potatoes, rich with goat cheese and caramelized onions; meaty dishes like dry-aged rib eye with Bandera butter and porterhouse pork chops with piloncilla rub; delicious breads, including buttermilk-nut mash biscuits, Mary Lou's hot-water cornbread, and butterscotch rolls; and enticing desserts like cajeta ice cream sandwiches and Shirley Rooney's apricot fried pies. ✪ Like the character of trail-driving cowboys, the spirit of this food is hearty, solid, and comforting. And like the photographs and stories of these cowboys offered throughout the book, the food is meant to make you feel that goodness endures. At the same time, the recipes are user-friendly—never complicated or laborious—and each is accompanied by information about the ingredients, an interesting tidbit or morsel of trivia, or a quick hint. ✪ In reading our book, you'll find yourself entertained by the rich and revered textures of the Chisholm Trail and Old West that weave themselves throughout the heritage of the Lone Star State. At the same time, you'll see how this kind of richly crafted trail cuisine is destined to claim its own place in modern Texas history. ✪ *Grady Spears and June Naylor, Fort Worth, Texas, 2003*

1

JUST FOR STARTERS

THE PLEASURE OF A GREAT MEAL is extended if you begin with appetite-teasers. Cowboys working the trail might have had to settle for a piece of jerky while they waited for the chuck-wagon cook to get their evening's stew ready, but we are blessed with an abundance of options today. ✪ The tamale is one of the greatest staples to come from Mexican cooking. It makes an excellent appetizer, although Grady has been known to eat nearly a dozen for a meal. Varieties of this treasured, rustic peasant food range from the soft, almost puddinglike tamal, which is steamed inside plantain leaves in Costa Rica, Guatemala, and some Caribbean island countries, to the sturdier, corn husk–wrapped tamale found throughout Mexico, New Mexico, and Texas. A true Tex-Mex menu always includes tamales. ✪ The tamale evolved from a bundle the Aztec people were making five hundred years ago using ground corn as the outer layer of the creation. The Aztecs placed great value on this food, presenting it to their gods during religious ceremonies. This might explain how the making and giving of tamales became a Mexican tradition at Christmas. The practice is so widespread today that people all over the Lone Star State give tamales to family and friends for the holidays. ✪ The luckiest tamale cooks in Texas grew up with an *abuela* (that's a grandma, to you gringos) who passed along a passel of valuable family secrets that resulted in gloriously flavored, picture-perfect tamales. The rest of us had to learn the particulars of this art form by trial and error, which usually required a great measure of humor. In this chapter, we offer some of Grady's signature tamales. We combine loads of flavor with some of the best tamale-making advice we've gathered from Mexican cooks over the years. ✪ We also offer suggestions for appetizers that will feed a crowd or a small dinner party. You'll find familiar favorites like Frito pie and fried oysters, as well as some delicious offerings from Grady's restaurants and his days spent working in the Big Bend region of far West Texas.

Grady's Basic Tamale

Makes 36 tamales

Here's a simple, all-purpose recipe to keep on hand for making tamales at the holidays, or any time of year. Tamales make a great appetizer, or you could serve them with a Caesar salad topped with drunken beans or pair them with grilled meat or fish for a main course.

PAGE 16
"Come and Git It!" [Cowpunchers "Hightailing it in to Chuck" with One Horse Pitching on Extreme Left], Three Block Ranch, New Mexico. 1909.

PREVIOUS SPREAD
The LS Outfit at the Chuck Wagon Having Dinner in the Shade of a Tree. LS Ranch, Texas. 1907.

4	CUPS *MASA HARINA*
3	CUPS CHICKEN STOCK, WARMED
2	CUPS LARD
3	TABLESPOONS VEGETABLE OIL
2	RED BELL PEPPERS, SEEDED AND DICED
4	JALAPEÑOS, SEEDED AND MINCED
1	RED ONION, DICED
2	CUPS FRESH CORN KERNELS
1/2	CUP CHOPPED CILANTRO
	KOSHER SALT
	ABOUT 50 CORN HUSKS, SOAKED IN WARM WATER
6	CORN HUSKS, SOAKED IN WARM WATER (or butcher twine)

Put the *masa harina* in a large bowl and reconstitute by adding warm chicken stock. Beat with a wooden spoon until the dough is stiff but smooth. Add a little more stock if necessary, but be sure to keep the mixture firm.

In another large bowl, beat the lard with a mixer fitted with a paddle until it is very fluffy, about 3 minutes. Continue to beat at a medium speed and add the *masa* a little at a time until well combined. The texture should be kept light and fluffy. To see if the mixture is blended well enough, drop a teaspoon of the dough into a glass of water. If it floats, it's mixed well. If not, keep beating. Set aside.

Heat the oil in a large skillet over high heat and cook the bell peppers, jalapeños, and onion for 4 to 5 minutes, or until the mixture begins to soften. Add the corn and cilantro, season with salt, and remove the pan from the heat. Gently fold mixture into the prepared *masa* until well combined, being careful not to overwork.

Choose several softened corn husks and tear into 72 thin strips. These will be used to tie the tamales. On a clean, dry surface, spread out 42 softened corn husks and spoon approximately 2 to 3 tablespoons of the prepared *masa* into the middle of each husk. Roll each tamale lengthwise, tightly, then twist at both ends, much like the wrapper of a Tootsie Roll. Securely tie each end with a strip of the corn husk or butcher twine. Set aside.

Prepare a steamer or a pot with a steaming rack, cover, and steam the prepared tamales for approximately 1 hour, or until the tamale is firm to the touch. Remove and serve warm with your favorite filling (see the next three recipes) or let cool, wrapped well in plastic, and freeze for future use.

Tamales Stuffed with Roasted Garlic Shrimp

Makes 36 tamales

Grady's signature tamale is served in a decorative way. We keep it in its husk with the ties on the ends but slit the middle open to spoon in the filling. The husk becomes the tamale's own little serving container.

2   TEASPOONS CUMIN SEEDS

1/4   CUP VEGETABLE OIL

2   RED ONIONS, DICED

6   JALAPEÑOS, SEEDED AND MINCED

4   ROMA TOMATOES, DICED

3/4   CUP RED CHILE SAUCE (page 131)

1/4   CUP ROASTED GARLIC

2   POUNDS PEELED, DEVEINED MEDIUM SHRIMP,
     COARSELY CHOPPED

1/2   CUP CHOPPED CILANTRO

     KOSHER SALT

36   GRADY'S BASIC TAMALES (page 20)

Preheat the oven to 400°F. Put the cumin seeds on a baking sheet and toast for 4 to 5 minutes, but watch carefully because they can burn quickly. Remove from the oven and cool.

Prepare the shrimp filling by heating the oil over high heat in a medium skillet and sautéing the onions and jalapeños for 3 to 4 minutes, or until they being to soften. Add the cumin seeds, tomatoes, chile sauce, and garlic,

stirring for 2 to 3 minutes, or until the sauce begins to thicken. Lower the heat to a simmer, add the shrimp, and cook for 5 to 6 minutes, stirring occasionally, until the shrimp are firm. Stir in the cilantro, season with salt, and remove from the heat.

Prepare each tamale by making a slit from one tied end to the other. Using both hands, push each end of the tamale toward the middle to form a pocket in the center. Spoon the filling evenly into each tamale and serve warm.

ROASTED GARLIC (makes 1/2 cup)

1   HEAD GARLIC

Preheat the oven to 400°F. With a sharp knife, slice off the pointed end of the head of the garlic, exposing the ends of the cloves. Wrap garlic loosely in heavy-duty foil and bake for 45 to 60 minutes, or until cloves feel soft to the touch. Remove from the oven and cool. Squeeze each clove to force the roasted meats out. Mash in a bowl until it forms a paste.

TEXAS COWBOY KITCHEN BITE

The most essential tamale ingredient is the *masa*, a dough made from sun- or fire-dried corn kernels that are also used to make corn tortillas. After the dried kernels have been soaked in lime water, they are ground into the substance called prepared *masa* that you can find in Mexican groceries or the Mexican section of supermarkets. Add lard (the preferred ingredient) or vegetable shortening to the *masa*. The fat is an essential ingredient for smooth, creamy, flavorful tamales.

Barbecued Quail Tamales with Avocado Cream

Makes 36 tamales

For this recipe, you can substitute chicken leg and thigh meat if quail isn't available. Don't skip the avocado cream, as it provides just the right balance to the barbecued quail.

BARBECUED QUAIL

3	TABLESPOONS VEGETABLE OIL
2	POUNDS BONELESS SKINLESS QUAIL MEAT
1/4	CUP RED CHILE SAUCE (page 131)
1/4	CUP BARBECUE SAUCE (page 145)
3	ROMA TOMATOES, DICED
1/4	CUP CHOPPED CILANTRO
	KOSHER SALT

AVOCADO CREAM

1	CUP CRÈME FRAÎCHE (page 144) OR SOUR CREAM
1/4	CUP HEAVY CREAM
4	RIPE AVOCADOS, PEELED AND COARSELY CHOPPED
	JUICE OF 1 LIME
	KOSHER SALT

36	GRADY'S BASIC TAMALES (page 20)

Prepare the quail by heating the oil in a large skillet over high heat. Sauté the quail meat for 5 to 6 minutes, or until the meat begins to brown, stirring occasionally. Stir in the chile sauce, barbecue sauce, and tomatoes, cooking for 5 to 6 minutes, or until the liquid starts to thicken. Add the cilantro, season with salt, and remove from heat.

Prepare the avocado cream by combining the crème fraîche, heavy cream, avocados, and lime juice in a food processor fitted with a metal blade. Process on a low speed until smooth and creamy. Season with salt and refrigerate for 10 minutes.

Prepare each tamale by making a slit from one tied end to the other. Using both hands, push each end of the tamale toward the middle to form a pocket in the center. Spoon the filling evenly into each tamale, top with avocado cream, and serve.

TEXAS COWBOY KITCHEN BITE

Great news: Tamales freeze really well! After you've steamed the entire batch, let the tamales cool completely. Place them by the dozen or half-dozen in resealable heavy plastic freezer bags. They'll keep in the freezer for a couple of months. To reheat, you have a couple of options: Open the bag about a quarter of the way and warm the tamales in the microwave, or simply steam them again. It's important that you use a wet reheating method. Throwing them in a hot oven doesn't work.

Chorizo and Oven-Dried Tomato Mash Tamales

Makes 36 tamales

Chorizo brings punch to this tamale, then you mellow the works out with the roasted tomatoes. If you don't want to dry your own, sun-dried tomatoes from your local grocer will work just fine.

2	TABLESPOONS VEGETABLE OIL
2	POUNDS SIMPLE CHORIZO (page 101)
1/4	CUP VEGETABLE OIL
1	CUP OVEN-DRIED TOMATOES (page 140)
1/2	CUP CHOPPED CILANTRO
1/2	CUP GRATED ASIAGO OR PARMESAN CHEESE
2	JALAPEÑOS, SEEDED AND DICED
36	GRADY'S BASIC TAMALES (page 20)

Prepare the chorizo by heating 2 tablespoons of vegetable oil in a large skillet and browning the chorizo for 10 to 12 minutes, stirring occasionally so that it doesn't stick to the pan. Remove the skillet from heat, drain the fat, and set aside.

Prepare the oven-dried tomato mash by combining the 1/4 cup of vegetable oil, tomatoes, cilantro, asiago, and jalapeños in a food processor fitted with a metal blade. Pulse until fairly smooth, then remove the mash and fold into the prepared chorizo. Stir the chorizo and mash over medium heat for, 4 to 5 minutes or until well combined and warm throughout.

Prepare each tamale by making a slit from one tied end to the other. Using both hands, push each end of the tamale toward the middle to form a pocket in the center. Spoon the filling evenly into each tamale and serve warm.

Zack T. Burkett, LS Foreman, Overlooking the Canadian River, Texas. 1907.

TEXAS COWBOY KITCHEN BITE

To steam tamales, load them with open tips facing up into a tamale steamer (found at a Mexican grocery) or a pot. Put the top on and let the bundles steam. Meanwhile, break out the coffee or beer and visit with your tamale-making pals. You'll want your favorite friends and family members helping with this project.

Pushcart Taquitos con Pork Picadillo

Makes 12 taquitos

Just across the Rio Grande from Texas, in towns such as Ojinaga, Boquillas, and Acuña, vendors sell a wonderful assortment of edibles from pushcarts. This border-town street food is some of our favorite eating, and it's easy to make at home.

3	TABLESPOONS VEGETABLE OIL
12	3-INCH WHITE CORN TORTILLAS
	(large tortillas may be cut down with biscuit cutter or soup can)
1	POUND PORK BUTT, DICED
1	WHITE ONION, DICED
4	CLOVES GARLIC, CHOPPED
3	JALAPEÑOS, SEEDED AND DICED
1/4	CUP TOMATO PASTE
1/4	CUP RED WINE VINEGAR
1/4	CUP CHOPPED CILANTRO
	KOSHER SALT
1	CUP JOSE FALCÓN'S SLAW (page 147)
1	CUP GRATED CACIOTTA OR MONTEREY JACK CHEESE

Heat the oil in a deep skillet over high heat. Fry each tortilla round for 3 to 4 seconds on each side, remove, and drain on paper towels. Cover with a towel to keep from drying out.

In the same oil, cook the pork for 8 to 10 minutes over medium heat, or until the pork is just starting to brown. Remove from heat, drain the fat, and return to the pan, boosting heat to medium high. Add the onion, garlic, and jalapeños, cooking for 3 to 4 minutes, stirring occasionally. Add the tomato paste and vinegar, cooking for an additional 5 to 6 minutes, or until the liquid starts to thicken. Stir in the cilantro, season with salt, and remove from heat. Divide the picadillo into the tortillas and top with Jose Falcón's Slaw and cheese.

Texas Goat Cheese Sliders with Creamed Onion Jam

Makes 12 sliders

Nope, these aren't oysters, which are the Louisiana version of sliders; these are baby burgers we call sliders because they go down so easy—especially with an ice-cold brew.

2 1/2	**POUNDS GROUND CHUCK**
3/4	**CUP GOAT CHEESE**
3/4	**CUP CREAMED ONION JAM (page 137)**
2	**TABLESPOONS KOSHER SALT**
1	**TABLESPOON COARSELY GROUND BLACK PEPPER**
12	**FRESH BISCUITS OR MINI HAMBURGER BUNS**

Prepare a grill to medium-high heat. In a large mixing bowl, combine the ground chuck, goat cheese, creamed onion jam, salt, and pepper. Using your hands, blend thoroughly. Divide the mixture into six patties, making sure they are firm and compact. Place the patties on the grill (or a hot skillet) and cook for 7 to 8 minutes on each side, or until done to the temperature you like. Serve hot on biscuits with more creamed onion jam.

Frito Pie with Venison Chili, Fancy Cheeses, and Texas Pico

Makes 6 to 8 servings

This is one of our all-time favorite Texan treats. We've dressed up this version with venison or quail chili, but you can use beef, too. The caciotta (or Monterey jack) and goat cheeses add sophistication to the flavor, and the Texas Pico makes a colorful finish with the rich topping of crème fraîche.

VENISON OR QUAIL CHILI

4	TABLESPOONS VEGETABLE OIL
1	RED ONION, CHOPPED
1	TABLESPOON MINCED GARLIC
2	POUNDS COARSELY GROUND VENISON OR DICED BONELESS QUAIL MEAT
1	CUP RED CHILE SAUCE (page 131)
1	TABLESPOON PURE CHILE POWDER (ancho or New Mexico is good)
2	TEASPOONS DRIED OREGANO
2	TEASPOONS GROUND CUMIN
2	TOMATOES, COARSELY CHOPPED
3	CUPS CHICKEN STOCK
	KOSHER SALT

TO ASSEMBLE

1	LARGE (16-ounce) BAG OF FRITOS
	TEXAS PICO (page 156)
2	CUPS SHREDDED CACIOTTA OR MONTEREY JACK CHEESE
1	CUP CRUMBLED GOAT CHEESE
2	CUPS CRÈME FRAÎCHE (page 144) OR SOUR CREAM

Prepare the chili by heating the oil in a stew pot or Dutch oven over medium heat. Add the onion and garlic, and sauté until soft. Add the venison and cook until starting to brown, stirring as necessary. Add the red chile sauce, chile powder, oregano, cumin, and tomatoes. Stir well to combine. Cook for 5 minutes, then lower the heat to a simmer and add the stock. Simmer the chili, uncovered, for 45 minutes to 1 hour. Stir occasionally to prevent sticking. Season with salt to taste. Remove from heat and set aside until ready to assemble the Frito pie. If preparing ahead of time, place the chili in an airtight container and refrigerate until ready to use.

Assemble the Frito pies by piling the Fritos into serving bowls. Top with the hot chili, pico, and cheeses. Drizzle with crème fraîche.

Dr Pepper-Marinated Skirt Steak Tostadas

Makes 8 tostadas

Dr Pepper—the soft drink originally made in Waco, where the Chisholm Trail crossed the Brazos River—is the perfect marinade for the peasant cut of beef called skirt or flank steak.

1	POUND SKIRT OR FLANK STEAK
1	16-OUNCE BOTTLE DR PEPPER
3	TABLESPOONS VEGETABLE OIL
8	CORN TORTILLAS
	KOSHER SALT
2	TABLESPOONS ALL-AROUND BEEF RUB (page 155)
1 1/2	CUPS GRATED CACIOTTA OR MONTEREY JACK CHEESE
1/2	CUP GOAT CHEESE
1	CUP JOSE FALCÓN'S SLAW (page 147)

In a large glass or ceramic casserole dish, combine the skirt steak and Dr Pepper for 4 to 12 hours in the refrigerator. When you're ready to cook, heat the oil in a large skillet over medium-high heat to 375°F. Fry each tortilla for 8 to 10 seconds on each side, remove from the skillet with tongs, season with salt, and let drain on a paper towel–lined plate.

Prepare a hot grill. Remove the marinated skirt steak from the Dr Pepper and coat in the beef rub. Grill the meat for 3 to 4 minutes on each side, or until desired temperature is reached. Remove the skirt steak from the grill and let rest for at least 5 minutes before slicing.

To assemble the tostadas, preheat the oven to 350°F. Place the tortillas on cookie sheets and sprinkle evenly with the cheeses. Slice the skirt steak against the grain into thin strips, about 1/2 inch wide, and evenly distribute between the tortillas. Bake for 5 to 6 minutes, or until the cheeses have melted just to bubbling. Remove from the oven and top each tostada with a spoonful of Jose Falcón's Slaw. Serve immediately.

Branding Scene, Spur Ranch, Texas. ca. 1910.

CHISHOLM TRAIL BIT

"It was a profession that engendered a pride. They were laborers of a kind, it is true, but they regarded themselves as artists, and artists they were. The cowboy was the aristocrat of all wage earners."

J. Frank Dobie

Guy Lee's Pan Del Campo with Cheese and Greens

Makes 8 servings

Here's the original cowboy flatbread, cooked during the trail era in a skillet over an open fire. Today we like to use the legendary Guy Lee's version as a cracker-crisp foundation for a rich, saladlike appetizer.

1	POUND (about 20 slices) BACON
1	CAN OF 8 REFRIGERATED BISCUITS
1/2	CUP ALL-PURPOSE FLOUR, SIFTED
1	CUP CILANTRO-NUT MASH (page 141)
4	RIPE ROMA TOMATOES, SLICED INTO THIN ROUNDS
3	CUPS GRATED MONTEREY JACK CHEESE
1 1/2	CUPS GOAT CHEESE
2	CUPS FIELD GREENS, WASHED AND PATTED DRY

Preheat the oven to 375°F. In a heavy skillet, cook the bacon until very crisp (fry in batches if necessary, to prevent overcrowding). Drain on paper towels, crumble, and set aside.

Remove the biscuit dough from the can and cut or pull apart into 8 equal pieces. Sprinkle some flour on a clean, dry work surface, flour a rolling pin, and roll each of the dough pieces out to approximately 9-inch rounds; don't worry about making them too thin, because the thinner they are, the crisper, lighter, and better they'll be. Carefully transfer them to baking sheets and bake for 10 minutes or until browned. Remove from oven.

Increase the oven temperature to 400°F. Spread each crust with some of the cilantro-nut mash and cover evenly with crumbled bacon, tomatoes, and cheeses. Return to the oven for 2 to 3 minutes, or until the cheese has melted. Remove and garnish with the field greens. Serve immediately.

2

SOUPS, SALADS, AND SIDES

TRAIL DRIVERS AND OTHER COWBOYS didn't have anything approaching the luxury of multicourse meals, something even the most casual diner in Texas takes for granted today. Had the coosie, the nickname given to the chuck-wagon cook, asked cowpokes if they would like a salad or soup before their entrée, he would have no doubt been strung up from the nearest hanging tree. Those trail drivers would have thought that their coosie had gone plumb crazy. ✪ We're certain, however, that chuck-wagon cooks were nothing if not creative and adventurous. Stories are legendary about the wonders these early chefs would work with practically nothing. We have to assume that if given the resources, their works could have been as lusty and indulgent as the mashed potatoes with goat cheese and caramelized onions or the warm spinach salad with deviled nuts, blue cheese, and bacon dressing. ✪ When preparing these soups, salads, and sides, keep in mind that just because they don't sound like appetizers, it doesn't mean they can't be served as such. Even dishes like Caesar salad with barbecued quail can be prepared and served in small portions, as can our Pinto Bean Chowder. Remember, these items are appetite-teasers and palate temptations that will get your guests excited about what's coming to the table next. Of course, you'll find some of them so irresistible that you'll find yourself wanting to make an entire meal out of them. ✪ A few good rules of thumb will help you make every dish sing. Always use the freshest ingredients possible and resist every urge to take shortcuts. If the recipe calls for thick-cut, wood-smoked bacon, be sure to find it. And remember to always, always read completely through the directions before working on a dish. Nothing's more frustrating than getting halfway done and realizing you have to go back to the store for a forgotten ingredient. ✪ And be thankful for such pleasures. Cowboys got to eat one or two offerings a day on the trail, if they were lucky.

Bacon-Wrapped Asparagus

Makes 4 servings

Dressing up otherwise plain vegetables always makes eating your healthy, green foods more appealing. Crisp asparagus is good anyway, but we don't think there's much that bacon can't improve.

1	POUND ASPARAGUS, TRIMMED
8	SLICES THICK-CUT, WOOD-SMOKED BACON
1/4	CUP BUTTER
	JUICE OF 2 LIMES
	KOSHER SALT

Preheat the oven to 350°F. In a large pot of water, blanch the asparagus over medium-high heat for 2 to 3 minutes, or until the spears can just be pierced with a fork tine. Remove, drain, and cool.

Partially cook the bacon in a skillet over medium heat. Remove from heat and transfer bacon to a paper towel–lined plate to drain and cool. Divide the asparagus into four bunches and wrap each bunch with 2 pieces of bacon, folding the ends of the bacon under to secure. Place in a foil-lined roasting pan, divide the butter by putting a smudge on each bundle of asparagus tops, and pour the lime juice over the asparagus. Season with salt and bake for 5 to 6 minutes, or until the asparagus reaches your desired tenderness.

PAGE 35
The OR Outfit Having Dinner in the Hot Noonday Sun. OR Ranch, Arizona. 1909.

PREVIOUS SPREAD
A JA Cook Inspecting His Stew, JA Ranch, Texas. 1908.

Smoky Caesar Salad with Barbecued Quail

Makes 4 to 6 servings

Here's a Caesar salad any cowpoke would love. We like topping it with barbecued quail, which is plentiful in Texas and available from specialty butchers elsewhere. If you absolutely can't find quail, use the meat from chicken legs and thighs—it's richer and more flavorful.

8	QUAIL, QUARTERED
1	CUP BARBECUE SAUCE (page 145)
2	TABLESPOONS OLIVE OIL
	SALT AND PEPPER

SALAD

2	HEADS ROMAINE LETTUCE, ROUGHLY CHOPPED
1	CUP GRATED ASIAGO CHEESE
3	CUPS CAESAR CROUTONS (page 149)
1 1/2	CUPS SMOKY CAESAR SALAD DRESSING (page 148)
	SALT AND PEPPER

Prepare the quail by placing it and half of the barbecue sauce, olive oil, and salt and pepper in a shallow baking dish, making sure all of the meat is coated well. Cover and marinate in the refrigerator for at least 6 hours but no more than 12 hours. When ready to cook, discard the excess marinade.

Grill the quail for 2 to 3 minutes on each side over medium-high heat, basting with remaining barbecue sauce. Remove quail when done and set aside, loosely covered, to keep warm.

Prepare the salad by tossing the lettuce, cheese, and croutons with the dressing until well combined. Season with salt and pepper. Divide the salad among plates. Top each salad with equal portions of the warm quail and serve immediately.

Spinach Salad with Deviled Nuts, Blue Cheese, and Bacon Dressing

Makes 8 to 10 servings

If you think you don't like spinach, you probably haven't tried anything like this spinach salad. Made rich with fancy cheeses, spicy nuts, and bacon, it's almost a meal in itself.

1	TABLESPOON VEGETABLE OIL
2	POUNDS BACON, DICED
1	RED ONION, DICED
2	TEASPOONS MINCED GARLIC
1/2	CUP CIDER VINEGAR
1/4	CUP BROWN SUGAR
2	CUPS CRUMBLED BLUE CHEESE
1	POUND FRESH BABY SPINACH LEAVES, WASHED AND PATTED DRY
	KOSHER SALT AND COARSELY GROUND BLACK PEPPER
1	PINT CHERRY TOMATOES, STEMMED AND HALVED
2	CUPS DEVILED NUTS (page 153)
1	CUP GRATED CACIOTTA OR MONTEREY JACK CHEESE

In a large skillet, heat the oil. Add the bacon and cook until well browned, draining as you go, to make sure the bacon isn't sitting in too much grease. Remove the cooked bacon from the pan with a slotted spoon and transfer to a paper towel–lined plate. Using the same pan, cook the onion and garlic over medium-high heat until they begin to soften. Add the cider vinegar and brown sugar, and simmer over medium-high heat until the sugar has completely dissolved. Remove from heat and add the blue cheese and half of the bacon, mixing well, to form the dressing. Place the spinach leaves in a large bowl. Pour the warm dressing over the spinach and toss lightly until well coated. Season with salt and pepper to taste. Divide the warm salad among 6 plates. Finish the salad by dividing the remaining bacon, cherry tomatoes, deviled nuts, and cheese on top of each salad. Serve warm.

CHISHOLM TRAIL TIME LINE

1866 Jesse Chisholm cut the trail by carting a heavy load of buffalo hides from Oklahoma to Kansas.

1870 In this single year, 300,000 Longhorns were herded northward through Fort Worth.

1877 All terminals were closed to the Texas cattle trade due to a so-called Texas Fever or Spanish Fever tick that the Texas beasts often carried. Although not harmful to the hearty Longhorns, this tick was deadly to weaker northern breeds.

1877 By this year, more than 5 million head of cattle had been driven through Fort Worth, but the arrival of the T&P Railroad in Fort Worth meant that it was cheaper to move cattle by rail, and the cattle drive era began to disappear.

1887 John Peter Smith, Morgan Jones, and J. W. Burgess obtained a charter to build a stockyards north of downtown and raised $200,000 to build the Fort Worth Union Stockyards, which opened in 1889.

1896 The last herd of cattle left the trail.

1901 America's two largest meat-packing companies agreed to build regional plants in the stockyards. Swift & Co. won a coin toss for land on the southern hillside of Exchange Avenue and Armour & Co. took the northern half. The plants opened in November 1902.

Maple Mashed Sweet Potatoes

Makes 6 to 8 servings

The perfect side dish for Braised Pig Trotters (page 100), these mashed potatoes also go well with Pat's Lamb Chops with Orange–Fig–Pecan Relish (page 103), your mom's Thanksgiving turkey, or your grandma's Easter ham.

4–6   LARGE SWEET POTATOES OR YAMS, PEELED AND CUT INTO CHUNKS

6   CLOVES GARLIC, PEELED

1   CUP BUTTER

1   CUP MAPLE SYRUP

KOSHER SALT AND COARSELY GROUND BLACK PEPPER TO TASTE

In a large pot, cover the potatoes and garlic with water and boil for 30 to 40 minutes, or until soft. Remove the pot from the heat and drain. Put the potatoes and garlic in a food processor, mixer, or food mill and process with the butter, syrup, salt, and pepper until blended well. Serve warm.

Goat Cheese and Caramelized Onion Mashed Potatoes

Makes 6 servings

Try these mashed potatoes with anything from a spice-rubbed steak to grilled vegetables. Our favorite goat cheese comes from Paula Lambert's Mozzarella Company in Dallas, but any quality goat cheese will work if you can't find Paula's.

2	POUNDS RUSSET POTATOES, PEELED AND CUT INTO 1¹/₂-INCH PIECES
6	CLOVES GARLIC, PEELED
1/3	CUP UNSALTED BUTTER
3/4	CUP HEAVY CREAM
	KOSHER SALT AND FRESHLY GROUND PEPPER
1	CUP GOAT CHEESE
1/2	CUP CARAMELIZED ONIONS (page 136)

Place the potatoes and garlic cloves in a large, heavy saucepan and cover with cold water. Over high heat, bring the water to a boil. Lower the heat to medium, cover the pot, and cook the potatoes until they are just soft when tested with the tip of a knife, about 20 minutes.

While the potatoes are cooking, heat the butter and cream over medium heat in another saucepan. Reduce by one-fourth.

In a colander, strain the water from the potatoes and garlic. While still hot, pass them through a food mill or a ricer with the butter and cream. Add salt and pepper, fold in the goat cheese and onions, and serve warm.

Green Chile–Cheese Grits

Makes 8 to 10 servings

Adding chile and cheese to grits has become the Texas way to improve on one of the best dishes to come out of the Old South. This comfort dish is so good you'll be tempted to eat the whole pan all by yourself, but if you decide to share, you can pair it with grilled pork chops or roasted trout ranchero for a great supper.

1	TABLESPOON BUTTER
2	ROASTED GREEN CHILES, SEEDED, AND CHOPPED (page 133)
1/2	CUP ROASTED GARLIC (page 21)
3/4	CUP CHOPPED CILANTRO
1-2	FRESH JALAPEÑOS, STEMS AND SEEDS REMOVED, MINCED
6	CUPS WATER
1 1/3	CUPS HOMINY GRITS
3	EGGS, BEATEN
3/4	CUP BUTTER
1	CUP GRATED SHARP CHEDDAR CHEESE
1	CUP GRATED CACIOTTA OR MONTEREY JACK CHEESE
	KOSHER SALT AND GROUND WHITE PEPPER

Preheat the oven to 350°F. Butter a 13 by 9-inch casserole dish and set aside.

In a blender or food processor, combine the chiles, garlic, cilantro, and jalapeños. Process until smooth. Set aside.

In a large pot, bring water to a boil, add grits, and stir well. Lower the heat to low and stir while the grits thicken. When the mixture is thick, remove from heat. Stir in the eggs, adding slowly, followed by the butter, cheeses, and the chile mixture. Add salt and pepper to taste. Pour the mixture into the prepared casserole dish and bake for 45 minutes.

Trail herd, somewhere in Texas. 1905–1912.

CHISHOLM TRAIL BIT

Jesse Chisholm, the man for whom the famous trail was named, was half-Cherokee, half-Scottish Indian trader, guide, and interpreter from Tennessee. Chisholm moved to the Cherokee tribal lands on the Arkansas River, married a Creek Indian, and was believed to have spoken fourteen Indian languages. Often an interpreter at treaty councils in Texas, Oklahoma's Indian Territory, and Kansas, Chisholm never drove cattle. Ironically, the historic figure for whom a restaurant would be named, suffered death by food poisoning at a trading post in Oklahoma in 1868.

Green Bean–Chayote Squash Casserole with Fried Onion Strings

Makes 6 to 8 servings

Green-bean casserole is just about everybody's holiday favorite, and this one gets a little extra color and texture from the light green chayote squash. Chayote, which was popular with the native Indians of Mexico, is shaped sort of like a pear and tastes a little like zucchini. For added comfort, we put Fried Onion Strings (page 48) on top.

CASSEROLE

1	POUND FRESH GREEN BEANS, ENDS TRIMMED
1/2	POUND FRESH CHAYOTE SQUASH, PEELED, SEEDED, AND JULIENNED
2	TABLESPOONS BUTTER
3	TABLESPOONS VEGETABLE OIL
1	POUND BACON, DICED
3/4	CUP DICED RED ONION
1/4	CUP UNSALTED BUTTER
1/4	CUP ALL-PURPOSE FLOUR
1 3/4	CUPS HEAVY CREAM
	KOSHER SALT AND FRESHLY GROUND BLACK PEPPER
1 1/2	CUPS GRATED ASIAGO CHEESE

Prepare the casserole by blanching the green beans and chayote in a large pot of water for 5 minutes. Remove from the heat and drain in a colander. Set aside to cool.

Meanwhile, butter a shallow 4-quart casserole or a 13 by 9 by 2-inch glass baking pan with butter and set aside.

Preheat the oven to 350°F. Heat the oil in a large skillet over medium heat. Add the bacon, stirring as necessary to separate the pieces so they cook evenly. Drain the grease as it accumulates so that the bacon won't be swimming in grease. When the bacon is half cooked, add the onion and continue to cook, stirring occasionally, until the bacon is done and the onion is soft. Transfer to the buttered casserole dish. Set the mixture aside.

In a separate pan, heat the unsalted butter over medium heat. Whisk the flour into the butter to create a roux, and cook for several minutes until the roux becomes fragrant but does not brown. Add the cream slowly while whisking to prevent lumps. Adjust the heat so that the sauce is simmering, not boiling, add salt and pepper, and cook for about 5 minutes, or until thickened. Put the green beans and chayote squash into casserole dish and cover with white sauce. Top with the grated cheese and place in the oven to bake for 20 to 25 minutes, or until the mixture is bubbling.

Remove the casserole from the oven and top with the warm, crispy, fried onion strings. Serve immediately.

Fried Onion Strings

Makes 8 servings

These crunchy tendrils are the perfect topper to our Green Bean–Chayote Squash Casserole (page 46). We'd even go as far as putting them on meatloaf sandwiches or in fish tacos.

1	**RED ONION, PEELED AND SLICED INTO THIN RINGS**
1	**CUP BUTTERMILK (or enough to cover the onions)**
1/2	**CUP BASIC SEASONED FLOUR (page 130)**
1	**CUP PEANUT OIL**

Prepare the fried strings by separating the slices of onion into rings and placing in a shallow bowl. Pour the buttermilk over the onion rings and let them soak for 30 minutes to 1 hour. Put the seasoned flour on a plate. Pour the oil into a skillet and heat to about 375°F over medium heat, using a thermometer to gauge heat. Drain the onion rings on paper towels and then dip them into the seasoned flour. Shake off any excess flour and slide the rings into the hot oil. Do not crowd the pan; cook the onions in several batches. Fry the strings until golden brown. Remove them as cooked and place on fresh paper towels to drain.

Bread Salad with Oven-Dried Tomatoes and Cheeses

Makes 8 servings

The idea for this comfort salad comes from the Italian *panzanella,* and we think it's a great way to use day-old bread. Easy and quick, it gets a rich topping of goat cheese and is great alongside any of your favorite cuts of grilled beef.

1/2   **CUP OLIVE OIL**

2   **CUPS GRATED ASIAGO OR PARMESAN CHEESE**

2   **TEASPOONS FRESH GARLIC, MINCED**

     JUICE OF 3 LIMES

6   **CUPS DAY-OLD FRENCH OR SOURDOUGH BREAD, CUT INTO LARGE CUBES**

2   **CUPS OVEN-DRIED TOMATOES** (page 140)

3/4   **CUP RED ONION, THINLY SLICED**

1   **LARGE HEAD ROMAINE LETTUCE, WASHED AND TORN INTO LARGE PIECES**

     KOSHER SALT AND FRESHLY GROUND COARSE BLACK PEPPER

1   **CUP CREAMY GOAT CHEESE**

In a large bowl, combine the oil, cheese, garlic, and lime juice, mixing well. Add the bread and toss to coat. Add the tomatoes, onion, and romaine, gently tossing to coat the lettuce. Sprinkle in salt and pepper, and top each salad with dollop of goat cheese and serve.

Mac and Texas Cheeses with Roasted Chiles

Makes 6 to 8 servings

Eating mac and cheese is about as good as getting a big hug from your favorite grandma—it just makes you feel happy inside. We like the smoky punch that the roasted chiles give this mac and cheese dish, which has been a big hit at Grady's restaurants.

4	POBLANO CHILES
1	CUP PLUS 1 TABLESPOON UNSALTED BUTTER
2	CUPS HEAVY WHIPPING CREAM
1	CUP MILK
1/2	CUP ALL-PURPOSE FLOUR
3	CUPS GRATED CACIOTTA OR MONTEREY JACK CHEESE
1	CUP GOAT CHEESE
	KOSHER SALT
1 1/2	POUNDS COOKED MACARONI
1	CUP SEASONED BREAD CRUMBS
2	CUPS GRATED ASIAGO OR PARMESAN CHEESE

ROASTED CHILES

Preheat the oven to 500°F. Place the chiles on a greased baking sheet and cook, using tongs to turn the chiles after about 8 to 10 minutes, so that they blacken evenly on all sides. When blackened, remove from the oven and seal the chiles inside plastic bags for 10 minutes. Remove the chiles from the bags and slip off the blistered skins. When cooled, remove the seeds and stems and cut into strips.

MAC AND CHEESE

Lower the oven temperature to 375°F. Using 1 tablespoon of the butter, grease a medium casserole dish and set aside.

In a saucepan, heat the cream and milk over medium-high heat. In a separate saucepan, melt the remaining butter over medium heat. Whisk the flour into the melted butter, stirring over medium heat for approximately 1 minute. Slowly pour in the heated whipping cream, whisking the mixture until it thickens. Remove the saucepan from the heat and stir in the caciotta and goat cheese. Season with salt and set aside. In a large mixing bowl combine the macaroni, cream mixture, and green chiles, mixing gently until well combined. Pour the macaroni into the greased baking dish and evenly spread the bread crumbs and grated asiago cheese over the top. Bake for 50 to 60 minutes, or until the top is browned.

Pinto Bean Chowder

Makes 4 to 6 servings

Lots of Texas families have a lifelong habit of cooking a big pot of beans on weekends. When you have beans left over, this is a great recipe that will add a whole new meal to your weekly menu. Serve with a big pan of Blue Ribbon Cornbread (page 168).

Ga'nt Horse in Big Country [on Canadian River Range, Texas].

MEMORIES OF OLD-TIME COWBOYS AND CHISHOLM TRAIL

Where is now that one familiar
  Chisholm Trail,
Winding northward sure and slow;
Gone forever—destroyed
  by progress,
Gone to realms of long ago.

Never more will bold trail bosses,
With their brave and
  dauntless bands;
Guide the restless Longhorns,
Through the Texas border lands.

Yes, the cowboys' trails are over,
And the dim trail gone at last.
But his name will be transmitted,
From the borders of the past.

H. H. Halsell, 1939

1	CUP CORN, CUT FRESH FROM THE COB
2	TABLESPOONS VEGETABLE OIL
1	CUP DICED BACON
2	CARROTS, DICED
4	CELERY STALKS, DICED
1	RED BELL PEPPER, DICED
2	YELLOW ONIONS, DICED
4	JALAPEÑOS, SEEDED AND DICED
6	CLOVES GARLIC, THINLY SLICED
2	CUPS COOKED PINTO BEANS, DRAINED
2	CUPS CHICKEN STOCK
	KOSHER SALT
1/2	CUP CHOPPED CILANTRO
6	TABLESPOONS CRÈME FRAÎCHE (page 144)

In a sauté pan, cook corn over high heat 4 to 5 minutes, until blackened, stirring occasionally. Set aside.

In same skillet, heat the oil and cook the bacon over high heat until it starts to brown. Add the carrots, celery, bell pepper, onions, jalapeños, and garlic, cooking until they begin to soften. Remove from heat.

In a food processor, puree half the beans with 1/2 cup of the chicken stock. Add processed bean mixture, remaining chicken stock, and remaining beans to the vegetables in the skillet, and simmer for 15 to 20 minutes. Season with salt to taste. Stir in the cilantro, remove from heat, and divide among bowls. Garnish with dollop of crème fraîche.

Corn-Tomato Bisque

Makes 4 servings

Nothing's better in summer than fresh corn and tomatoes from the farmers market, and few soups are easier to make than this one. It's rich enough to make a meal, alongside the warm Spinach Salad (page 41). Add a bit of chopped fresh jalapeño on top if you want to give the creamy flavor a kick.

3	TABLESPOONS BUTTER
1	MEDIUM-SIZE WHITE ONION, CHOPPED
3	CLOVES GARLIC, MINCED
1½	CUPS CORN, CUT FRESH FROM THE COB
2	POUNDS RIPE ROMA TOMATOES, PEELED AND COARSELY CHOPPED
2	TABLESPOONS CHOPPED FRESH OREGANO
1	SPRIG FRESH THYME
2	TABLESPOONS DRY WHITE WINE
	KOSHER SALT AND FRESHLY GROUND BLACK PEPPER
1½	CUPS HEAVY CREAM
	UP TO 1 CUP CHICKEN STOCK (optional)
2	TABLESPOONS GRATED MONTEREY JACK CHEESE
3	TEASPOONS CUMIN SEEDS, LIGHTLY TOASTED
¼	CUP CHOPPED CILANTRO

In a medium-size pot, melt the butter over low heat. Add the onion and garlic. Sauté just until tender, about 10 minutes. Do not allow to brown. Add the corn, tomatoes, oregano, thyme, and wine. Simmer for about 20 minutes, stirring occasionally. Add salt and pepper.

Puree the mixture in batches in a blender or food processor (or if you have a handheld immersion blender, puree the mixture in the pot). Return the mixture to the pot and add the cream. If the soup is too thick, add a little warm chicken stock. Reheat but do not allow the mixture to boil.

Divide evenly among bowls and scatter the cheese, cumin seeds, and cilantro on top.

Lone Star and Molasses Baked Beans

Makes 6 to 8 servings

No Texas barbecue is complete without baked beans, and these beans have a whole lot more flavor than most. Lone Star is a great beer for sipping, and it combines well with the brown sugar and molasses to give the beans a new flavor variety.

1	TABLESPOON BUTTER
2	TABLESPOONS VEGETABLE OIL
2	CLOVES GARLIC, MINCED
2	RED ONIONS, DICED
2	POUNDS BACON, DICED
6	JALAPEÑOS, SEEDED AND MINCED
2	RED BELL PEPPERS, DICED
1	BOTTLE LONE STAR BEER
1	CUP BARBECUE SAUCE (page 145)
1	CUP BROWN SUGAR
1/4	CUP MOLASSES
4	CUPS COOKED PINTO BEANS, DRAINED
	KOSHER SALT

Preheat the oven to 375°F. Grease a 13 by 9-inch casserole dish with butter and set aside.

In a large sauté pan, heat the oil. Sauté the garlic and onions until they start to soften, then add the bacon, jalapeños, and bell peppers, stirring occasionally, cooking until the bacon has browned. In a large bowl, combine the beer, barbecue sauce, brown sugar, and molasses, mixing well. Add the beans and bacon mixture, and season with salt to taste. Transfer to prepared casserole dish and bake for 45 minutes, or until bubbling and browned on top.

Cabbage Braised in Texas Port

Makes 6 servings

Llano Estacado is one of Texas's growing number of wineries that produce a good port wine. It's the perfect cooking ingredient for this version of a warm slaw, which tastes great—and, because of its rich purple color, looks good, too—when paired with pork chops, pork tenderloin, or any game.

2	TABLESPOONS VEGETABLE OIL
1	POUND BACON, DICED
1	RED ONION, THINLY SLICED
2	TABLESPOONS MINCED GARLIC
3	CUPS SHREDDED RED CABBAGE
1	CUP PORT WINE
2	TABLESPOONS BROWN SUGAR
	KOSHER SALT

Heat the oil in a large, deep-sided skillet and cook the bacon for 3 to 4 minutes over medium-high heat, until it begins to brown. Add the onion and garlic, cooking for 2 to 3 minutes, or until they begin to soften. Add the cabbage and sauté for 4 to 5 minutes over medium-high heat, tossing occasionally. Add the port and sugar, stir well, and lower the heat to medium. Cook uncovered for 20 minutes, or until most of the liquid is absorbed. Season with salt to taste and serve.

Spoonbread with Simple Chorizo

Make 8 servings

Spoonbread has been popular throughout the South for centuries, thanks to the ever-available cornmeal. It makes a satisfying substitute for potatoes or rice at any meal, but we especially like it with smoked ham or brisket.

1	TABLESPOON BUTTER
4	CUPS MILK
2	CUPS CORNMEAL
	KOSHER SALT
2	TEASPOONS BAKING POWDER
1/4	CUP UNSALTED BUTTER, MELTED
4	EGGS, BEATEN UNTIL THICK
1 1/2	CUPS GRATED MONTEREY JACK CHEESE
1	POUND COOKED SIMPLE CHORIZO (page 101)
1	TABLESPOON ROASTED GARLIC (page 21)

Preheat the oven to 375°F and grease a medium-size casserole dish with the butter. In a saucepan, over medium-high heat, bring the milk to a boil. Gradually add the cornmeal, stirring constantly until all the milk has been absorbed. Remove from heat and let cool. In a large bowl, combine the cornmeal mixture, salt, baking powder, and butter until well mixed. Gently fold in the eggs, cheese, chorizo, and garlic. Pour into the casserole dish and bake for 20 to 30 minutes, or until the top starts to brown. Remove and serve warm.

3

THE TEXAS CHEF'S CORRAL

In this chapter we've rounded up some of our favorite Lone Star cooking compadres and asked them to share some wonderful recipes from their days and nights on the Texas trail. ✪ In these pages, you'll find a salad from Paula Disbrowe, a cowgirl cuisine star in Austin, and savory scones from Rebecca Rather, whose bakery on Fredericksburg's Main Street has created quite a happy stir among locals and tourists alike. Meanwhile, Jeff Blank from Hudson's on the Bend in Austin is sure to wow you with his watermelon-laced pork tenderloin. ✪ A smoky potato salad recipe comes from Dan Potter, a noted radio personality in Fort Worth, and a sumptuous crawfish tamale recipe was created just for this book by Angele Stavron, whose Hot Damn, Tamales! has revolutionized the contemporary tamale industry. Bruce Auden, the inventor of extraordinary food at Biga on the Banks in San Antonio, contributes smoked salmon chowder, and David Garrido, of Jeffrey's in Austin, promises to bust your buttons with his paella and chile-fueled red snapper. ✪ Matt Martinez, Jr., a cuisine colleague from Dallas, shares his family's down-home chalupa recipe, a staple at his El Rancho restaurants in Austin and Dallas for more than forty years. We also feature biscuits from Paula Lambert, whose Mozzarella Company in Dallas has become an international institution in cheese-making. ✪ We saved the sweetest stuff for last, of course: Shirley Rooney, who worked with Grady years ago at the Gage Hotel in Marathon, offers a treasured brownie recipe, and the *Fort Worth Star-Telegram*'s Art Chapman says his sweet potato–pecan pie recipe is perfect for those who want to suffer just the tiniest degree of pain when they've finished. ✪ No guts, no glory, we say. A little discomfort is a small price to pay when the reward is a wealth of great grub from such a talented lot of inspired creators from across Texas.

Matt's Famous Austin-Style Chalupas

Makes 4 servings

An owner of Tex-Mex restaurants in Austin and Dallas, Matt Martinez, Jr., loves to share his passion for what many fellow Texans consider the ultimate comfort food. He says Tex-Mex is the source of severe longings because our bodies crave that gratifying combination of carbohydrates and protein, offered in abundance in this easy recipe for perfectly simple chalupas.

2	CUPS MATT'S REFRIED BEANS
8	CRISP CORN TOSTADAS
2	CUPS SHREDDED MONTEREY JACK CHEESE
3	CUPS CHOPPED LETTUCE
1	CUP COARSELY CHOPPED TOMATO
2	CUPS SHREDDED BRISKET OR CHICKEN
	CHOPPED WHITE ONION AND FRESHLY SLICED
	JALAPEÑO, FOR GARNISH

Preheat the oven to 375°F. Distribute the refried beans evenly over each tostada. Top with the cheese and bake until the cheese melts. Remove from the oven and top with lettuce, tomato, and brisket. Serve with garnishes.

MATT'S REFRIED BEANS

1/4	CUP BACON DRIPPINGS
4	CUPS COOKED PINTO BEANS
	SALT AND PEPPER

In a heavy skillet, heat the drippings until smoking hot. Add 1 cup of the pinto beans, heat for 1 minute, then carefully mash together with the drippings. Lower the heat and add the remaining beans, cooking and mashing, 1 cup at a time, over low heat, until smooth.

MATT MARTINEZ, JR.

Matt's food roots are traced to the renowned El Rancho restaurant in Austin, where his grandpa opened the Capital City's first Tex-Mex eatery after fighting in Pancho Villa's army. Matt, who loves cooking in his cast-iron skillet, has become an ambassador for the cult-revered cuisine that is Tex-Mex by helping restaurateurs from countries as distant as Russia learn how to make this distinctive fare. "Tex-Mex is the fastest growing ethnic cuisine in the world!" Matt crows. "Just look at London and Paris. There are more Tex-Mex restaurants in those cities than any other kind of Mexican restaurant."

PAULA DISBROWE

After a career in New York as a food and travel writer for *Food & Wine*, *Restaurant Business*, *Fortune*, and the *New York Times*, Paula shifted gears, put on a cowboy hat, and went back to cooking. Her résumé includes cooking at a château in the South of France, and at an agriturismo, a farmhouse bed-and-breakfast in Tuscany. Her experience enables her to combine her healthful Mediterranean cuisine with the big, robust flavors of the Texas Hill Country, an ideal combination for Hart & Hind Fitness Ranch near the Frio River.

Cowboys of the Matador Ranch Taken by Flashlight. Second from Left, back row, is John Jackson, Wagon Boss. Matador Ranch, Texas. 1907.

Golden Beet, Celery, and Chevre Salad

Makes 4 servings

Cowgirl chef Paula Disbrowe says that she's uniquely qualified as a chef at a fitness ranch because she's such a salad freak. This particular creation, which is great for lunch or as a first course at dinner, is all about contrasts. "With the clean-tasting celery, sweet roasted flavor of the beets, and creamy goat cheese, even the most macho of cowboys have been seduced by this rather feminine combination," she promises.

4	GOLDEN BEETS WITH GREENS ATTACHED, TRIMMED (see below) AND CLEANED
2	SPRIGS FRESH THYME
	SEA SALT AS NEEDED
4	TABLESPOONS GOOD-QUALITY EXTRA-VIRGIN OLIVE OIL, PLUS EXTRA FOR SPRINKLING ON RAW BEETS
	JUICE OF 1 LARGE LEMON
1	TABLESPOON CHAMPAGNE VINEGAR
1	HEAPING TABLESPOON DIJON MUSTARD
2	TEASPOONS MEXICAN MINT MARIGOLD OR TARRAGON, CHOPPED
	SPRINKLING OF CRUSHED RED PEPPER FLAKES (if desired)
	KOSHER SALT AND FRESHLY GROUND PEPPER
1	LARGE BUNCH ORGANIC CELERY, CLEANED AND TRIMMED
4	OUNCES CHEVRE CHEESE

Preheat the oven to 350°F. Prepare the beets by trimming the stems down to ¼ inch. (Leave a portion of the stem attached during the roasting process to retain moisture and avoid excess bleeding of color.) Wash the beets, using a vegetable brush to remove any grit. Trim the bottom "tail" of the beets. Toss the beets with the thyme sprigs, sea salt, and a sprinkling of olive oil. Wrap in foil, place on a cookie sheet, and roast until tender when pierced with a knife—about 1 ½ hours. If possible, allow beets to cool in their foil packet. Peel the beets and slice into rounds.

Meanwhile, trim the beet leaves from their stems, wash, and blanch in boiling water. Shock the greens in ice water, drain (using paper towels to squeeze excess moisture from leaves), chop, and set aside.

To make the vinaigrette, whisk together the lemon juice, vinegar, mustard, olive oil, marigold, red pepper, salt, and pepper in medium-size bowl. When ready to serve the salad, shave the celery into thin slices. Toss the celery and the chopped beet greens with half the vinaigrette. Toss the beet rounds with the remaining vinaigrette. Divide the celery among four salad plates, and top with equal portions of beets and a crumbling of chevre cheese.

Angele's Mudbug Mollies

Makes 48 tamales

Angele Stavron's Hot Damn, Tamales! might be the best-tasting tamales on the entire planet. We're crazy for her wild mushroom–goat cheese and her poblano-chicken tamales, but she's really outdone herself with this crawfish creation. Serve these with our Texas Pico (page 156) or Tart Black Bean Salsa (page 119).

ANGELE STAVRON

So how did a nice Greek girl from Cowtown wind up making some of the most famous tamales in the nation? Let's just say it was a long, strange trip that included stints as a musician in rock, country, and punk bands. While living in Austin as a practicing vegetarian, Angele was dismayed at the lack of tamales that didn't include lard in the masa, so she made her own. Hot Damn, Tamales!—an eatery featuring tamales crafted with vegetable shortening and exotic ingredients—was launched in Austin in 1997 and moved to Fort Worth in 1999. They've been featured in the *New York Times* and on NBC's *Today Show*. Angele has been known to send her tamales to customers across the United States using overnight mail. She even has Hollywood celebrities among her clientele, but she doesn't ship and tell.

2	CUPS VEGETABLE SHORTENING
6	CUPS *MASA HARINA*
2	TABLESPOONS GROUND CHILE POWDER
2	TEASPOONS GROUND CUMIN POWDER
3	TABLESPOONS KOSHER SALT
2	TABLESPOONS BAKING POWDER
4 1/2	CUPS WARM WATER OR CHICKEN BROTH
56	HUSKS, SOAKED IN WARM WATER TO SOFTEN

Cream the shortening in the bowl of an electric mixer with the paddle attachment fixed and at low speed. Add the *masa harina* and mix just until blended. Add the spices, salt, and baking powder. When these are well mixed, slowly add the liquid to the masa mixture and beat until the masa is smooth and all is well incorporated.

Choose 8 softened corn husks and tear each into 12 thin strips to make 96 ties for your 48 tamales. On a clean, dry surface spread out 48 softened corn husks and spoon 2 to 3 tablespoons of the prepared masa into the middle of each husk. Roll each tamale lengthwise, tightly, then twist at both ends, much like the wrapper of a Tootsie Roll. Securely tie each end with a strip of the corn husk or butcher twine and set aside.

Prepare a steamer or a pot with a steaming rack, cover, and steam the prepared tamales for approximately 1 hour, or until the tamale is firm to the touch. Remove and prepare each tamale by making a slit lengthwise from one tied end to the other. Using both hands, push each end of the tamale toward the middle to form a pocket in the center. Fill each evenly with the Mudbug Mollies or other favorite filling and serve warm. Once cool, the unfilled tamales can also be wrapped in plastic and sealed inside self-closing freezer bags for future use.

MUDBUG MOLLIES FILLING

1/2	CUP BUTTER
1/4	CUP OLIVE OIL
1	ONION, CHOPPED
2	RED BELL PEPPERS, SEEDED AND CHOPPED
2	GREEN BELL PEPPERS, SEEDED AND CHOPPED
3	CLOVES GARLIC, MINCED
1	POUND CRAWFISH MEAT AND TAILS
	KOSHER SALT AND FRESHLY GROUND BLACK PEPPER

In a skillet melt the butter and oil. Add the onion and sauté until they're translucent. Add the peppers and garlic, and sauté until done. Add the crawfish and cook 5 minutes more. Season with salt and pepper. Set aside until serving time.

Applewood–Smoked German Potato Salad

DAN POTTER

A morning news anchor and *Hello, Texas* show host for WBAP radio in Dallas–Fort Worth, Dan Potter is a passionate cook who shares his recipes in a segment he calls "Dining with Dan." What listeners don't know about the award-winning journalist is that his passion for music is traced to his longtime involvement with Drum Corps International and Bands of America. He's known as an accomplished gourmet among friends and family.

Makes 4 servings

Perfect with roasted chicken, barbecued brisket, or grilled steaks, this is one of many specialties created by Dan Potter of WBAP radio in Fort Worth. Dan likes to use a stovetop smoker when making these potatoes and recommends buying the applewood chips made specifically for indoor smokers that are typically sold at gourmet cooking stores.

2	TABLESPOONS APPLEWOOD CHIPS
4	LARGE RUSSET POTATOES, SCRUBBED, SKINS ON, SLICED 1/4-INCH THICK
2	TEASPOONS KOSHER SALT
5	SLICES BACON
3	CLOVES GARLIC, CHOPPED
2	LARGE SHALLOTS, PEELED AND SLICED
1/4	CUP CIDER VINEGAR
1/2	CUP CHICKEN STOCK
2	TABLESPOONS CHOPPED CHIVES
	KOSHER SALT AND PEPPER

Place the wood chips on the bottom of a stovetop smoker. Place the drip pan over the wood chips and the rack on top of the drip pan. Arrange the potato slices on the rack and sprinkle with salt. Put the top on the smoker and place it over a burner on medium-low heat. Cook for 45 to 50 minutes, or until the potatoes are done but still firm. When the potato slices are done, place them in a bowl and prepare the dressing.

In a sauté pan, cook the bacon over medium heat until crisp. Remove the bacon strips, drain on paper towels, and set aside, leaving the rendered bacon fat in the pan. Increase the heat to medium high and add the garlic and shallots. Sauté for 1 minute. Increase the heat to high and add the vinegar. Boil until the vinegar has reduced by one-third.

Add the chicken stock and reduce the sauce by one-third. Once the chicken stock has been reduced, pour the contents of the sauté pan over the potatoes and add the chopped chives and salt and pepper. Crumble the bacon and add to the bowl. Mix until the potato slices are coated well. Serve warm.

Cheddar and Black Pepper Biscuits

Makes 12 to 16 biscuits

Paula Lambert of the Mozzarella Company in Dallas says, "I'm sure that every household in the South has its own favorite biscuit recipe. I like this one because of the smooth rich cheese and the fiery spice of the black pepper." We couldn't agree more. Try these with Bruce Auden's Smoked Salmon Chowder (page 73) or sliced and filled with smoky ham swabbed with spicy brown mustard.

PAULA LAMBERT

Entrepreneur cheese-maker extraordinaire, Paula founded her small cheese factory in 1982 in Dallas because she sorely missed the fresh mozzarella she'd come to love while living in Italy. In the ensuing years, the Mozzarella Company has won coveted awards and become a fixture in gourmet shops and restaurants and hotel kitchens throughout the United States and Mexico City and aboard South African Airlines. Her cornucopia of cheese products has been featured in national magazines, served at the Academy Awards and to presidents and royalty, and has made Paula a member of the James Beard Foundation's Who's Who of Food and Beverage in America. Paula's recipes are found in *The Cheese Lovers Cookbook*, her first and fabulous effort.

1	TABLESPOON UNSALTED BUTTER, MELTED
2	CUPS UNBLEACHED ALL-PURPOSE FLOUR
1	TABLESPOON BAKING POWDER
1/2	TEASPOON SALT
1/3	CUP SHORTENING OR UNSALTED BUTTER
3/4	CUP BUTTERMILK
4	OUNCES CHEDDAR CHEESE, CUT INTO 1/4 INCH CUBES
1	TEASPOON FRESHLY GROUND BLACK PEPPER

Preheat the oven to 450°F. Line a baking sheet or a cake pan with parchment paper or lightly butter the surface with about 1 teaspoon of the melted butter. The choice of the pan will determine the outcome of the biscuit: For a crispy exterior, set the biscuits about 1/2 inch apart on a baking sheet. If you want moister, fluffier biscuits, place them close together in a cake pan. Select the pan of your choice and have it ready for the biscuits.

Combine the flour, baking powder, and salt in a bowl. Add the shortening and cut it into the dry ingredients using 2 knives, a pastry blender, or your hands. Work the shortening in well, until it is reduced to pea-size pieces. Add the buttermilk and mix briefly, just to incorporate it. It is very important not to overwork the dough, or the biscuits will not be delicate and light. Gently mix in the cheddar and black pepper. The dough will be fairly sticky.

Place the dough on a smooth, well-floured surface and pat with your hands to about 3/4 inch thick. Cut out the biscuits, using a 2-inch round glass or cookie cutter. Dip the cutter into flour between cuts to keep from sticking. Place the biscuits on or in the prepared pan. The remaining dough may be gently gathered together and rolled out again for more biscuits. Brush the tops with the remaining melted butter. Place the biscuits in the oven and bake for about 10 minutes, or until the tops are golden brown. Remove from the oven and serve warm.

Smoked Salmon Chowder

Makes 8 servings

Bruce Auden, whose dishes at San Antonio's Biga on the Banks are the stuff of national renown, brings together the fire of chiles and the smooth sophistication of salmon in this hearty soup. We think it's perfect as a meal in itself.

BRUCE AUDEN

Bruce won over Texas diners in 1991 when he combined classical techniques with exotic Mexican and Asian flavors at his tiny Biga on the Banks in San Antonio. Since then, his seasonal and daily menus have earned accolades from *Gourmet* and *Esquire* magazines, and he's been named a finalist for James Beard awards twice. One bite of his aged beef, seafood, and Texas game, and you'll be a follower, too.

"Pink" Murray, Wagon Boss of the OR Outfit, Telling His Men off for the Day's Work, OR Range, Arizona. 1909.

1	SWEET POTATO, DICED
1	YUKON GOLD POTATO, DICED
1/4	POUND APPLEWOOD SMOKED BACON, DICED SMALL
1/2	LINK DUCK SAUSAGE, DICED SMALL
1/2	WHITE ONION, DICED SMALL
1	CARROT, DICED SMALL
3	CELERY RIBS, DICED SMALL
1	POBLANO CHILE, DICED
2	SERRANO CHILES, DICED
1	RED BELL PEPPER, DICED
1	TABLESPOON MINCED GARLIC
2	TABLESPOONS TOMATO PASTE
1/2	CUP ALL-PURPOSE FLOUR
2	CUPS HEAVY CREAM
1	CUP CLAM JUICE
2	QUARTS CHICKEN STOCK
	JUICE OF 1 LEMON
	JUICE OF 1 LIME
1	BAY LEAF
1/3	BUNCH CILANTRO LEAVES
2	TABLESPOONS FRESH THYME
1/2	POUND DICED SMOKED SALMON
2	LARGE TOMATOES, DICED
1 1/2	TABLESPOONS CUMIN
1	TABLESPOON DRIED, GROUND ANCHO CHILE
1	TABLESPOON CHILE POWDER
	KOSHER SALT AND PEPPER

Cook the potatoes in boiling water until almost tender; strain. Shock in ice water, drain, and set aside.

Cook the bacon until crisp. Add the sausage and sauté several minutes, then add the onions, carrots, and celery. Cook until onions become translucent. Add the chiles, red bell pepper, and garlic, and sauté for an additional 2 to 3 minutes. Add the tomato paste and flour; continue stirring and add the heavy cream. Reduce until thick. Add the potatoes, clam juice, chicken stock, lemon and lime juice, bay leaf, cilantro, thyme, salmon, tomatoes, cumin, ancho chile, and chile powder. Salt and pepper to taste; serve warm.

Chicken Thighs Paella

Makes 4 servings

Inspired by the Spanish cuisine classic, David Garrido's paella takes a subtle boost from serrano chiles and gets a nice fluffiness from Texmati rice. This is comfort food, rest assured. We like it with a glass of dry, full-bodied Spanish rosé.

6	TABLESPOONS EXTRA-VIRGIN OLIVE OIL
4	CHICKEN THIGHS
	SALT AND PEPPER
2/3	CUP DICED ONION
6	CLOVES GARLIC, FINELY CHOPPED
2	SERRANO CHILES, STEMMED, SEEDED, AND FINELY CHOPPED
2	CUPS TEXMATI RICE
2	PINCHES SAFFRON THREADS
2	CUPS CHOPPED TOMATO
3	CUPS WATER
6	BAY LEAVES
2–3	TEASPOONS SEA SALT
4	LEMON WEDGES, FOR GARNISH

In a medium-size saucepan, heat the olive oil over medium heat. Season the chicken thighs with salt and pepper, and sear 4 to 6 minutes, or until golden brown. Add the onion, garlic, and serrano chiles, and cook for 2 to 4 minutes, or until the onion is translucent. Add the rice and sauté for 2 minutes, or until rice starts turning light brown. Add the remaining ingredients. When the mixture starts to boil, lower the heat to low and cook for 14 to 17 minutes, or until the rice is tender. Serve hot and garnish with the lemon wedges.

DAVID GARRIDO

David's official résumé says this star chef "possesses a pitch-perfect palate," and we couldn't have put it better. Born in Canada and raised by a Mexican diplomat in Mexico, Puerto Rico, and Costa Rica, David was educated in Switzerland. A frequent guest chef at the James Beard House in New York, David's work since 1991 at Jeffrey's in Austin has been lauded for his masterful blend of Southwestern and Latin flavors. His creations became such a favorite of George W. Bush's that David had to open a Jeffrey's in Washington, D.C., when the governor became the president.

Snapper with Ancho-Tomatillo Sauce

Makes 4 servings

Our buddy David Garrido exploded onto the Texas dining scene with his mega-hit Austin restaurant, Jeffrey's. This dish is one he created for his Jeffrey's at the Watergate, aimed to please homesick Texans living in our nation's capital. It's sure to please you, too.

4	TABLESPOONS OLIVE OIL
1/2	MEDIUM ONION, THINLY SLICED
1	SERRANO CHILE, MINCED
1	CLOVE GARLIC, MINCED
6	TOMATILLOS, HUSKED AND QUARTERED
2	ANCHO CHILES, STEMMED AND SEEDED
1	TABLESPOON LEMON JUICE
1/4	CUP VEGETABLE STOCK
1	CUP CHOPPED CILANTRO
	SALT
4	5-OUNCE BONELESS, SKINLESS SNAPPER FILLETS
3/4	CUP INEXPENSIVE WHITE WINE

Preheat the oven to 450°F. Heat 2 tablespoons of the olive oil in a medium-size skillet over medium heat. Add the onion and cook about 6 minutes, or until light brown. Add the serrano, garlic, tomatillos, anchos, lemon juice, and vegetable stock; lower the heat and simmer for 5 to 7 minutes or until the chiles are soft. Transfer the mixture to a blender, add cilantro, and puree until a smooth salsa is created. Salt to taste. In another medium-size skillet over high heat, heat the remaining 2 tablespoons of olive oil and carefully sear the snapper on both sides. Cook for 1 to 2 minutes, or until golden brown. Add the white wine and bake in the oven for 4 to 7 minutes, or until cooked through. Transfer the snapper fillets to 4 plates and garnish with the ancho-tomatillo salsa and Tart Black Bean Salsa (page 119).

Sweet Potato–Pecan Pie

Makes 8 servings

Art Chapman of the *Fort Worth Star-Telegram* is well known for his sweet potato–pecan pie, a Southern staple that's been made from hundreds of recipe variations passed among generations of family and friends. Art says that while some folks crumble the pecans, others carefully arrange pecan halves, and that it's okay to go as heavy or light as you like with the cinnamon, allspice, and nutmeg. "Some of the best pie-makers dare to use a ration of pure ribbon cane syrup," he says, "but be warned, the thick, molasses-like syrup is strong, and too much is really too much."

2–3	SWEET POTATOES, ENOUGH FOR ABOUT 1¹/₂ CUPS COOKED PULP (canned are okay)
1/4	CUP PACKED LIGHT BROWN SUGAR
3	EGGS
1	TABLESPOON HEAVY CREAM
1/4	TEASPOON EACH CINNAMON, GROUND ALLSPICE, AND GROUND NUTMEG
2	TABLESPOONS VANILLA EXTRACT
3/4	CUP PLUS 2 TABLESPOONS GRANULATED SUGAR
1	CUP LIGHT, DARK, OR BLENDED CORN SYRUP
1¹/₂	TEASPOONS UNSALTED BUTTER
	PINCH OF SALT
	PINCH OF GROUND CINNAMON
1	CUP PECAN HALVES
1	PIECRUST, HOMEMADE OR STORE-BOUGHT

Preheat the oven to 325°F. If using fresh sweet potatoes, peel and cook in boiling water, about 15 minutes, or until tender. Cool and drain well before mashing. In a large bowl, combine the sweet potatoes, brown sugar, one egg, cream, 1 tablespoon of the vanilla, and 2 tablespoons of the granulated sugar.

In another bowl, stir together the remaining vanilla, remaining 3/4 cup of granulated sugar, the corn syrup, 2 eggs, butter, salt, and the pinch of cinnamon, until the mixture becomes a slightly opaque syrup, about 1 minute. Stir in the pecans.

Line a deep 9-inch pie plate with pie dough. Spoon in the sweet potato filling evenly. Pour the pecan syrup on top and bake for 1¹/₂ to 1³/₄ hours.

ART CHAPMAN

 In his many years of traveling Texas as a *Fort Worth Star-Telegram* columnist, Art has had ample opportunity to sample the sensational eats indigenous to the Lone Star State. He can tell you about winning recipes for every cook-off held in the most remote corners of the state, and he can whip up a mean batch of jambalaya and osso buco, too. But it's his sweet potato–pecan pie that can bring tears of joy to a grown man. As Art so eloquently puts it, "Sweet potato–pecan pie is not a dainty dessert. It is a rich, thick pie you can feel slowly sludge through your veins. Your heart will grind into another gear, and your bottom will drop into the first available chair. You do not eat this pie if you plan to operate heavy equipment. A long, uninterrupted nap is the only antidote." Sounds like a perfect afternoon to us.

Before she had folks driving hundreds of miles across West Texas to her Burnt Biscuit Bakery in Marathon for one of her apricot fried pies, Shirley Rooney had folks driving similar distances for a slice of her exquisite buttermilk pie at the Gage Hotel, also in Marathon. A legend in Big Bend Country, Shirley says she can't ever bake pies when Grady is around. "He'd just eat them right up," she says, and there wouldn't be any left for paying customers.

Photo courtesy James Evans

Edwin Sanders (right) and Three Cowboys Taking Time out for a Game of Hearts, Three Circles Ranch, Texas. 1906.

West Texas Brownies

Makes 8 servings

Cowboys, ranchers, and Big Bend refugees will drive a hundred miles or more to satisfy a sweet tooth with treats from Shirley Rooney's Burnt Biscuit Bakery in Marathon. Be forewarned: Shirley's special cream–cheese brownies are addictive, so bake and eat at your own risk.

BROWNIE MIX

1/4	CUP BUTTER
2	OUNCES UNSWEETENED CHOCOLATE
2	EGGS
1/8	TEASPOON SALT
1	CUP SUGAR
1/2	TEASPOON VANILLA EXTRACT
1/2	CUP FLOUR

CHEESECAKE MIXTURE

8	OUNCES CREAM CHEESE, SOFTENED
2	TABLESPOONS MARGARINE, MELTED
1	TABLESPOON CORNSTARCH
1	CUP EAGLE BRAND SWEETENED CONDENSED MILK
1	EGG
1	TEASPOON VANILLA EXTRACT

ICING

1/3	CUP MARGARINE, MELTED
1/4	CUP COCOA
1/4	CUP MILK
1	CUP CONFECTIONERS' SUGAR
1	TEASPOON VANILLA EXTRACT
1/2	CUP CHOPPED PECANS

Prepare the brownie batter by melting the butter and chocolate in a double boiler. When cool, beat together by hand until color lightens and gradually add the eggs and salt, beating until well creamed. Add the sugar and vanilla, and beat well, then add the flour. Spray a 9 by 9-inch pan with nonstick spray and pour in the brownie batter. Set aside.

Preheat the oven to 300°F. Prepare the cheesecake layer by blending the cream cheese, margarine, cornstarch, and Eagle Brand milk until fluffy. Add the egg and vanilla, beating until smooth. Pour this mixture over the brownie layer in the pan. Bake for 50 minutes to 1 hour.

Prepare the icing by beating the margarine, cocoa, milk, confectioners' sugar, and vanilla together until smooth. When the brownie is baked, remove from the oven and spread the icing on top while the brownie is still hot and in the pan. Top with chopped pecan pieces and let stand until cool. Wrap in plastic wrapping and refrigerate overnight.

Bacon Cheddar Scones

Makes 8 scones

Here's a hearty element for a bountiful holiday brunch spread, thanks to the genius of Rebecca Rather. These are the perfect accompaniments to our Green Chile–Cheese Grits (page 45) or black bean soup. Like everything at Rebecca's Fredericksburg bakery, these are downright heavenly.

REBECCA RATHER

Praised as a pastry queen, Rebecca moved her repertoire of baking thrills from Austin to the Hill Country when she opened Rather Sweet Bakery in Fredericksburg. Folks from Austin and San Antonio plan day trips around journeys to Rebecca's bakery just for a taste of her key lime pie, strawberry ricotta cake, and cinnamon rolls. Weekend escapists find themselves returning time and again for Rebecca's sensational breakfast and lunch menus, too.

Photo courtesy Tracy Trahar Photography

2	CUPS ALL-PURPOSE BLEACHED FLOUR
2	TEASPOONS BAKING POWDER
1/4	TEASPOON SALT
1/2	TEASPOON PEPPER
1/8	TEASPOON SUGAR
1/4	CUP PLUS 2 TABLESPOONS UNSALTED BUTTER, CUT INTO SMALL CUBES
1	CUP GRATED CHEDDAR CHEESE
3	GREEN ONIONS, MINCED
2	JALAPEÑOS, SEEDED AND MINCED
5–6	SLICES OF BACON, COOKED AND CHOPPED INTO 1-INCH PIECES
1/2	CUP BUTTERMILK OR HEAVY CREAM
1	LARGE EGG
2	TABLESPOONS MILK

Preheat the oven to 350°F. Use a mixer with a paddle attachment to combine the flour, baking powder, salt, pepper, and sugar in a large bowl. While mixing on low speed, gradually add the cubes of butter until the mixture resembles small peas. Add the grated cheese and mix just until blended.

(This can also be done by hand: Stir together the flour, baking powder, salt, pepper, and sugar in a large bowl. Gradually cut in the butter with a pastry blender or two knives until the mixture resembles small peas. Stir in the cheese.)

Add the green onions, jalapeños, bacon, and 1/3 cup buttermilk to the flour mixture. Mix by hand just until all the ingredients are incorporated. If the dough is too dry to hold together, use the remaining buttermilk, adding 1 tablespoon at a time, until dough is pliable and can be formed into a ball. Mix as lightly and as little as possible to ensure a light-textured scone. Remove dough from the bowl and place it on a lightly floured pastry board. Pat the dough into a ball. Using a well-floured rolling pin, flatten the dough into a circle about 7 inches wide and 1/2 inch thick. Cut into 8 equal wedges.

Whisk the egg and the milk in a small mixing bowl to combine. Brush each wedge with the egg wash.

Place the scones on an ungreased baking sheet and bake for 18 to 20 minutes, or until golden brown and no longer sticky in the middle. Serve warm.

Pork Tenderloin with Watermelon Salsa

Makes 6 servings

Jeff Blank of Hudson's on the Bend, just outside Austin, created this wonderful summertime dish, he says, for "one of those evenings when you don't want to go inside and you're feeling just a little hungry. Barefoot children will soon be chasing fireflies, and it's a fine night for grilling."

JEFF BLANK

As the owner and executive chef of Hudson's on the Bend restaurant just outside Austin, Jeff has developed a specialized Hill Country cuisine that bears so much gusto a new term had to be coined. He and his partners call it Fearless Cooking, a concept bursting with flavor and passion. "This is not food for those afraid of flavor," Jeff says, "nor for the faint of heart." You'll find a treasure trove full of examples in the Hudson's cookbook, *Cooking Fearlessly*.

3	CUPS SEEDED AND DICED WATERMELON, TO YIELD 2 CUPS JUICE
3	JALAPEÑOS, INCLUDING SEEDS AND RIBS IF YOU LIKE MORE HEAT
1	TABLESPOON SALT
2	CUPS SUGAR
1/4	CUP MIDORI LIQUEUR
2	POUNDS PORK TENDERLOIN
	SALT AND PEPPER

Puree the watermelon and jalapeños in a blender. Strain mixture through a sieve and return to the blender. (If you won't be injecting the tenderloin, don't worry about straining the marinade.) Add the salt, sugar, and liqueur and blend for 2 minutes. Reserve 1 cup for basting. Draw the marinade up into a syringe-type injector. Poke and inject the marinade throughout the tenderloin. After marinating, season the meat with salt and pepper.

Prepare coals in a grill and plan to use the combination technique of direct and indirect heat. Roll the tenderloin over the direct heat to establish some sexy grill marks and then move it to a slower part of the grill to finish cooking. Baste the tenderloin periodically throughout the cooking process.

Cook the tenderloin to an internal temperature of 160°F. (Despite all the warnings from your mother about the need to cook pork to 170°F, the truth is 160°F will kill off anything that might harm you.) Allow the meat 5 minutes to rest, then slice into medallions. Fan across some Watermelon Salsa for a great summer meal. *Note:* For best results, inject the meat the day before and store in an airtight plastic bag with extra marinade.

WATERMELON SALSA

2	CUPS WATERMELON, SEEDED AND FINELY DICED
1	GRANNY SMITH APPLE, FINELY DICED
1	RED ONION, JULIENNED
2	CLOVES GARLIC, MINCED
1	MANGO, PEELED AND DICED
2	JALAPEÑOS, SEEDED AND FINELY DICED
1	BUNCH CILANTRO, LEAVES ONLY
2	TABLESPOONS SUGAR
	SALT AND PEPPER
	JUICE OF 2 LIMES
	SPLASH OF RICE WINE VINEGAR

Combine all ingredients and chill well.

4

FROM THE BUTCHER SHOP

COWBOYS WHO MADE a meager living pushing cattle up the long trail learned to live with a diet that consisted mostly of fried meat. Each morning, the coosie would cook hunks of meat in beef tallow, which the cowpokes would gobble with biscuits and coffee. Any variance was considered a treat, even if it was a vile-tasting stew with ingredients of undisclosed origin. ✪ It's a testament to the skill and knowledge of cattle raisers today—there are more than 150,000 of them in Texas alone—that beef has become such desirable fare. Americans' demand for beef has risen 25 percent since 1998, with consumers spending about $71 billion on beef in 2005. Consumption estimates, in fact, are that we eat nearly 67 pounds of beef per capita annually. Yep, beef is what's for dinner; it's probably for breakfast and lunch, too. ✪ Today this king of meats in no way resembles the tough Longhorns that those trail drivers ate day after day. Instead, we're treated to the luxury of choosing between three superior grades of meat, so ascribed by the USDA for the meat's color, firmness, texture, age, and marbling. It's that marbling, of course, that gives great flavor and juiciness. That's why prime-grade beef bears the most marbling and flavor, followed by choice and select. ✪ We are partial to rubs, as you'll see in this chapter. These seasoning blends don't tenderize the meat in any way but serve to bring out the natural flavors more dramatically. You can make a rub of brown sugar, salt, pepper, ground chiles, paprika, and dried oregano, store it in an airtight container, and use it for months on end to dress up chicken, pork chops, pork tenderloin, roasts, and steaks. ✪ Our butcher shop chapter also includes recipes for lamb and pork shanks. Shanks can be a little difficult to find but are worth the effort. Cowboys have always enjoyed eating pork and lamb when they were lucky enough to find it. You probably never knew how much you could enjoy other meats, but we think our pig trotters braised with rosemary and cinnamon or lamb chops slathered in honey, orange juice, and Dijon will convince you.

Buck Reams's Sourdough Chicken-Fried Steak

Makes 6 servings

Few things were more likely to please a cowboy than a good ol' chicken-fried steak. This recipe comes from our favorite chuck-wagon cook, Buck Reams, who's also a Texas singer. Don't worry if you don't have a batch of sourdough made up already—you can make a substitute batter from the one we use on onion rings (page 97). Good cuts of meat for chicken-fried steak include top round and rib eye.

2   CUPS BASIC SEASONED FLOUR (page 130)

2–3   CUPS BUCK'S SOURDOUGH STARTER (page 87)

4–6   CUPS PEANUT OIL, OR ENOUGH TO COMPLETELY COVER THE STEAKS IN THE DUTCH OVEN

6   TENDERIZED BEEF STEAKS, POUNDED THIN KOSHER SALT AND FRESHLY GROUND BLACK PEPPER

Place the seasoned flour in a shallow dish or on a plate. The flour should be heavily seasoned, not bland. Pour the sourdough starter into a wide, shallow bowl. Set aside.

Pour the oil into a Dutch oven or a heavy, deep-sided skillet and set the pan over a fire or on a stove over medium-high heat. Heat the oil to 375°F, using a thermometer to determine the temperature.

While the oil is heating, prepare the steaks by breading. It is helpful to use one "dry hand" and one "wet hand" while dipping the steaks. One at a time, dip a steak into the flour, then into the sourdough starter, completely coating the steak. Finally dip it into the flour once again, completely coating it. Set the prepared meat on a wire rack on a clean sheet pan until there are enough coated to fill the pan without crowding. When the correct temperature is reached, slide 2 or 3 steaks into the hot oil. Cook the steaks for 4 to 6 minutes, turning once, taking care not to break the coating. After the steaks are cooked, place them on a paper towel-lined sheet pan to drain. Repeat the cooking process, allowing the oil to come back to 375°F before adding the next batch of steaks. Cook the steaks as above. Season with salt and pepper while the steaks are hot. Serve immediately with gravy or ketchup.

Buck's Sourdough Starter

Makes 10 cups

This incredible starter is the key to a great chicken-fried steak, and you'll also use it in our Sourdough Flapjacks (page 170). Be sure to refrigerate any starter you don't plan to use soon. It will keep indefinitely if properly tended.

4	**CUPS WARM WATER**
1	**¼-OUNCE PACKAGE ACTIVE DRY YEAST**
1	**CUP SUGAR**
6	**CUPS ALL-PURPOSE FLOUR**

Fill a large crock or a large bowl with the water. Sprinkle the yeast over the top and let it dissolve for at least 4 minutes. Using a long spoon or a whisk, stir in the sugar and flour. Loosely cover with plastic wrap and set the mixture aside at room temperature for at least 12 hours before using it.

Once you begin using the starter, it must be "fed" and replaced. Do not finish it completely, but rather add the same proportions of water, sugar, and flour to the existing starter after taking some out.

For example, if you remove half of the starter, add back 2 cups warm water, ½ cup sugar, and 3 cups flour. Blend the new ingredients into the starter with a whisk and set aside.

TEXAS COWBOY KITCHEN BITE

Born on the cattle-driving trail, the Texas staple we know as chicken-fried steak was poor folks' food. The cowboys ate pretty much what their coosie could scare up. The Longhorn was a tough beef, so the coosie pounded it until tender with whatever tools he could find. Then he dredged it in flour and fried it up in a Dutch oven. Gravy helped stretch the meal even further, which continued to be an important effort during the Depression. The Texas Restaurant Association estimates that Texans order some 800,000 chicken-fried steaks daily, and that doesn't count what we eat at home!

Dry-Aged Rib Eye with Bandera Butter

Makes 4 servings

If you've never tasted a dry-aged steak, whoa—you're fixin' to be hooked. Dry-aged beef may be hard to find, but a good butcher will find it for you—and it's sold online, too. And here, we've named the butter "bandera," which means "flag" in Spanish, for the green cilantro, red oven-dried tomato, and white garlic that represent the colors of the Mexican flag. Like all the Cowboy Butter flavors (page 143), this one will keep in your freezer for use over the long haul.

2	TABLESPOONS VEGETABLE OIL
1 1/2	CUPS LIGHT BROWN SUGAR
1/4	CUP KOSHER SALT
1/4	CUP COARSELY GROUND BLACK PEPPER
4	16-OUNCE DRY-AGED RIB EYE STEAKS
1/4	CUP BANDERA BUTTER (page 143)

Prepare a hot grill. While the grill is heating, place the oil in one bowl and the sugar, salt, and pepper in another. Coat the steaks well in the oil, then place the steaks, one at a time, in the sugar mixture. Cover the steaks completely in the sugar and seasonings. When the grill is ready, cook the steaks to your desired temperature. Let the steaks rest for 5 minutes; serve topped with a dab of the Bandera butter.

You can also preheat your oven to 450°F. After coating the steaks in oil and seasonings, sear the steaks in a heavy skillet over high heat for about 2 to 3 minutes per side. Transfer the steaks to a baking sheet and bake for 5 to 10 minutes, or until they reach an internal temperature of 140°F. Remove from the oven, let stand for 5 minutes, then top with butter and serve.

Beef Short Ribs Braised in Port

Makes 6 servings

One Morning's Roundup of Hereford (white face) Cattle Coming into Camp. Shoe Bar Ranch, Texas. 1912.

Anytime we put these out on a buffet at a party, that's the first dish to go. The bones are cut short, and they're meaty and addictive. Whip up a batch of Green Chile–Cheese Grits (page 45) to go alongside; the spice and butter are a great foil to the sweet port on the ribs.

3 TABLESPOONS PEANUT OIL

5–6 POUNDS BEEF SHORT RIBS

1 LARGE YELLOW ONION, COARSELY CHOPPED

2 LARGE CARROTS, PEELED AND CHOPPED

2 CUPS BEEF STOCK OR BROTH

2 CUPS TEXAS PORT

KOSHER SALT AND FRESHLY GROUND PEPPER

2 TABLESPOONS COLD UNSALTED BUTTER, CUT INTO
4 OR 5 PIECES

Preheat the oven to 375°F. In a large, deep-sided skillet, heat the oil over medium-high heat. Cut the ribs into 2- to 3-rib sections. Brown the ribs on all sides in the hot oil without crowding the meat. Do this in batches if necessary. It should take about 5 to 7 minutes per batch. As the ribs are browned, transfer them to a roasting pan.

Add the onion and carrots to the skillet and sauté them in the same hot oil about 5 minutes, or until softened and beginning to brown. Pour the vegetables over the ribs in the roasting pan. Add the beef stock and port. Season the ribs with salt and pepper. Cover the pan and place it in the oven. Braise the ribs for about 2 1/2 hours, or until the meat is tender. Using tongs, remove the ribs from the cooking liquid and arrange them on a serving platter. Loosely cover the ribs with foil.

Strain the remaining liquid into a saucepan, reserving the vegetables. Put the vegetables on the serving platter along with the ribs. Place the saucepan with the cooking liquid over medium-high heat. Boil to reduce it by one-half. Remove the saucepan from the heat and whisk in the cold butter piece by piece. By whisking away from direct heat, the butter should emulsify rather than melt and separate in the sauce. Taste the sauce and adjust the seasoning with salt and pepper if necessary. Pour over the ribs and vegetables, and serve.

CHISHOLM TRAIL BIT

Spanish explorers, missionaries, and their settlers brought cattle and horses to this part of the New World. Over the next couple of hundred years, the animals, many of which had escaped or been abandoned, multiplied in staggering numbers on the grasses of the Gulf Coast prairies and South Texas plains. The cattle brought by Anglo settlers from the southeastern states resulted in a surplus of livestock in Texas by the mid-nineteenth century. Attempts to ship the creatures to markets across the ocean or to drive them to the South and to California didn't turn enough profit to be worth the trouble.

At the end of the Civil War, the Texas economy struggled, but Texans recognized the prospect of wealth on the hoof. Thousands of cattle had been left to graze wildly throughout the state during the war. Led by Joseph McCoy of Illinois, a group of budding entrepreneurs recognized an opportunity to make a fortune by meeting the new, growing demand for red meat. In Abilene, Kansas, McCoy in 1867 managed to convince buyers that the cattle should be driven north from Texas. Using an artery called the Chisholm Trail, this breed, still unfamiliar to the non-Texan, was brought slowly and steadily to market.

The best flavor in a steak, in our opinion, occurs when you cook the meat to a cooler temperature. Trust us, a rare or medium-rare steak is much more tender and tastes better than a steak that's cooked longer. Invest in a meat thermometer and see what we mean. For a rare steak, the temperature is 140°F, medium-rare is 145°F, medium is 160°F, and well-done is 170°F. Always let the steak "rest" by standing on a cutting board for 5 minutes after you've removed it from the oven or grill. It will cut more easily and better retain juices this way.

Beef Tenderloin with Hollandaise Diablo

Makes 8 to 10 servings

It's hard to believe that a dish that tastes this good and looks so impressive is the easiest thing in the world to make. To make sure you cook it precisely to the right temperature, you'll need a meat thermometer. Keep in mind that the smaller end of the tenderloin will be closer to medium to medium well and the big end will be medium rare.

1/4	CUP SALT
1/2	CUP COARSELY GROUND BLACK PEPPER
1	4- TO 5-POUND TENDERLOIN, TRIMMED
1/4	CUP VEGETABLE OIL
2	CUPS HOLLANDAISE DIABLO (page 138)

Preheat the oven to 500°F. In a mixing bowl, combine the salt and pepper and pour into a baking sheet. Roll the whole tenderloin in the pepper and salt mixture, so that the tenderloin is completely covered. In a large braising pan, heat the oil on high heat. Place the whole tenderloin in the hot oil and cook for 4 to 6 minutes on all four sides.

Remove from the heat and place the tenderloin on a baking sheet. Finish in the oven for 20 to 25 minutes, or until internal temperature is 140°F. Remove from the oven and let stand for 10 to 15 minutes. Slice into 8 to 10 pieces and serve with warm Hollandaise Diablo.

Glazed Rib Roast

Makes 6 servings

Our All-Around Beef Rub (page 155) will create a wonderful glazed shell around the meat. Your best bet for perfect results lies in using a convection oven to get the desired crust around the roast. Keep in mind that roast temperatures differ from steak temperatures: A rare to medium-rare roast will be 135°F, while 140° to 145°F is closer to medium well. A pork roast temperature should be 160°F. Always use an instant-read thermometer and do not let it touch the bone when taking a reading.

1   **BONE-IN TRIMMED RIB ROAST, EITHER BEEF OR PORK**
      (about 5 to 6 pounds)

1/2 **CUP PEANUT OIL**

2   **ONIONS, PEELED AND CUT INTO QUARTERS**
      ALL-AROUND BEEF RUB (page 155)

Preheat the oven to 500°F. Rub the roast on all sides with the oil. Select a roasting pan that will just hold the meat. Place the roast in the roasting pan and surround with the onion pieces. Pack the rub onto the roast, covering the top and sides completely. Place the meat in the oven and roast for 30 minutes.

Without opening the oven door, lower the heat to 325°F and continue to roast the meat for an additional 45 minutes to 1 hour, or until the internal temperature reaches 135°F. When the meat reaches the desired temperature, remove it from the oven and set aside, loosely covering with foil for about 20 minutes to allow the meat to rest and the juices to settle. At serving time, slice the meat between the rib bones and serve with the onions and any juices that have accumulated in the bottom of the pan.

Gonzales Meatloaf

Makes 6 to 8 servings

Because we like to make this flavorful meatloaf with Nolan Ryan's ground sirloin, we named it for the town close to Nolan's family ranch. If you like a spicy flavor, increase the amount of hot pepper sauce or add a few chopped fresh jalapeños. Just be sure to save the leftovers for meatloaf sandwiches the next day.

2	POUNDS NOLAN RYAN GROUND SIRLOIN
3	EGGS, BEATEN
1	CUP DRIED BREAD CRUMBS
4	CLOVES GARLIC, MINCED
1	RED ONION, CHOPPED
2	TOMATOES, SEEDED AND DICED
1/2	CUP CHOPPED CILANTRO
1/4	CUP WORCESTERSHIRE SAUCE
1 1/2	CUPS GRATED MONTEREY JACK CHEESE
2	TABLESPOONS HOT PEPPER SAUCE
1/2	CUP BROWN SUGAR
	KOSHER SALT

Preheat the oven to 350°F. In a large bowl, combine all the ingredients, mixing well. Place the mixture in a greased loaf pan. Bake for 45 minutes, then increase the heat to 425°F and cook for an additional 15 minutes, or until the meatloaf is firm to the touch. Remove and serve warm.

Calf's Liver with Sage-Buttermilk Onion Rings

Makes 8 servings

These are the best onion rings ever, thanks to a thin, crunchy crust that gets its lightness from club soda. Just be careful not to make the batter in advance, because the soda will go flat. They're the perfect topper to this serving of old-fashioned, sautéed calf's liver.

1	CUP BASIC SEASONED FLOUR (page 130)
3	POUNDS CALF'S LIVER, CUT INTO 1/2-INCH-THICK SLICES
3	TABLESPOONS PEANUT OIL

Place the flour in a wide, shallow bowl or oblong dish. Place the liver pieces in the seasoned flour, one piece at a time, dusting the liver well. Heat the oil in a large, heavy sauté pan or skillet. Sauté the liver over medium–high heat for 1 1/2 to 2 minutes per side.

SAGE-BUTTERMILK ONION RINGS

2	CUPS BUTTERMILK
6	EGGS, BEATEN
1	CUP CLUB SODA
4	1015 ONIONS (see page 217), SLICED INTO RINGS 1 INCH WIDE
2	CUPS BASIC SEASONED FLOUR (page 130)
4	TABLESPOONS FINELY CHOPPED FRESH SAGE
6	CUPS PEANUT OIL
	KOSHER SALT

Combine the buttermilk, eggs, and club soda in a bowl, mixing well. Soak each ring in the buttermilk batter for 5 to 10 minutes. In another large, shallow bowl, combine seasoned flour with chopped sage. Dredge the soaked rings in the sage-seasoned flour. If the batter doesn't adhere well, batter and flour again.

Heat 3 cups of the oil in a deep-sided skillet or Dutch oven to 375°F. Fry each onion ring for 3 to 4 minutes, turning once until golden brown. Remove, drain on paper towels, and season with salt. Cook in several batches, adding oil as necessary and allowing the oil to reheat to 375°F between each batch.

ONION RING VARIATIONS

SPICY ONION RINGS

Add 2 to 3 tablespoons hot pepper sauce to the sage-buttermilk mixture.

HONEY ONION RINGS

Add 1/4 cup honey to the sage-buttermilk mixture.

CUMIN ONION RINGS

Add 3 teaspoons ground cumin to the sage-buttermilk mixture.

"The few hundred thousand cattle of Spanish blood...which were multiplied until three and a half million head were estimated as Texas' belongins'. They had been somewhat improved in breed, but were still wiry, nervous, long-limbed creatures, with slender, branching horns and restless eyes. They could run like deer, and were almost as wild."

Charles Moreau Harger,
"Cattle Trails of the Prairies"
(Scribner's Magazine, 1892)

A Cross-B Cowpuncher [Frank Smith] Branding a Maverick in the Open Range with a Ring Branding Iron, Cross B Ranch, Texas. 1909.

Porterhouse Pork Chops with Piloncilla Rub

Makes 4 servings

Piloncilla is simply Mexican brown sugar, and finding it is easy if you have a Latin market nearby—just remember to look in the produce section; otherwise it's in the Mexican food section in mainstream markets. Piloncilla or another dark sugar makes a great glaze or searing rub for beef because when sugar melts, it creates a shell around the meat, ensuring that the meat stays moist and flavorful. Unlike brown sugar, which is granulated and has mild flavor, piloncilla comes in a cone and has a much more intense essence.

1	CUP PILONCILLA RUB (page 134)
1	TABLESPOON KOSHER SALT
2	TABLESPOONS GROUND CAYENNE PEPPER
1	TABLESPOON GROUND PAPRIKA
2	SPRIGS THYME, FINELY CHOPPED
2	TABLESPOONS VEGETABLE OIL
4	18-OUNCE PORK CHOPS

Prepare the grill. In a large, wide bowl, combine the piloncilla rub with the other seasonings and thyme. Brush the oil on the pork chops, then place the chops, one at a time, in the piloncilla mixture, turning to coat.

Cook the pork chops on a hot grill until their internal temperature registers 150° to 165°F on a meat thermometer. Serve warm.

Braised Pig Trotters

Makes 6 to 8 servings

From the moment Grady first served these, they have been a gigantic hit. The long, slow braising method used here turns the front pork leg into one of the most flavorful, tender meats you've ever wrapped your mouth around. Keep in mind that pork shanks are gigantic, so they may be hard to find. Make buddies with your local butcher and see if he can't round them up for you. Otherwise, you can easily substitute the more readily available lamb shanks.

6–8	18- TO 22-OUNCE PORK OR LAMB SHANKS
1 1/2	CUPS SEASONED FLOUR
1/2	CUP OIL
2	RED ONIONS, DICED
6	CARROTS, PEELED AND SLICED INTO 1/2-INCH-THICK ROUNDS
10	CLOVES GARLIC, PEELED
4	CUPS CHICKEN STOCK OR BROTH
2	CUPS WHITE WINE
1/2	CUP ROSEMARY, CHOPPED FROM STEM
1/2	CUP BLACK PEPPERCORNS
6	CINNAMON STICKS
1/4	CUP COLD BUTTER

Preheat the oven to 325°F. In a large bowl, coat the shanks with the seasoned flour. Heat the oil in a large roasting pan over two burners on your stovetop. Place the shanks in the pan and brown on all sides over high heat, 3 to 4 minutes on each side. Remove shanks from pan and set aside. In the same pan, add the onions, carrots, and garlic, and cook, stirring occasionally, about 10 minutes or until the onions are becoming soft. Return the shanks to the pan, add the stock, wine, rosemary, black peppercorns, and cinnamon sticks, and cook covered in oven for approximately 2 1/2 hours, or until pork is tender. Remove from the oven and strain the remaining liquid into a saucepan. Cook the liquid over high heat for 5 to 7 minutes, or until reduced by one-half. Whisk in the cold butter and remove the pan from the heat. Transfer the shanks to serving dishes and ladle the sauce over the top.

Simple Chorizo

Makes 2 pounds

Chorizo is a zippy Mexican sausage that makes excellent taco and tamale filling, and it's great with scrambled eggs and pan-fried potatoes for a hearty breakfast.

2	POUNDS GROUND PORK BUTT
2	TEASPOONS GROUND CORIANDER
4	TEASPOONS GROUND RED PEPPER FLAKES
2	TABLESPOONS GROUND CINNAMON
2	TEASPOONS DRIED OREGANO
1/4	TEASPOON GROUND CUMIN
2	CLOVES GARLIC, MINCED
	KOSHER SALT

Place all of the ingredients in a large mixing bowl. Using a large spoon or your hands, mix well to distribute all of the seasonings. If all of the chorizo is not called for in the recipe, package the chorizo in 1/2-pound packages. Extract all of the air and freeze for up to 1 month.

Use this in the recipe for Chicken Breast Stuffed with Chorizo and Fancy Cheese (page 123).

THE TEXAS COWBOY

"The Texans are perhaps the best at the actual cowboy work. They are absolutely fearless riders and understand well the habits of the half-wild cattle, being unequaled in those most trying times when, for instance, the cattle are stampeded by a thunderstorm at night, while in the use of the rope they are only excelled by the Mexicans."

Theodore Roosevelt, 1885

Pat's Lamb Chops with Orange-Fig-Pecan Relish

Makes 4 to 6 servings

Texas singer-songwriter Pat Green is a great friend, and he's passionate about cooking lamb chops. We've adapted his lamb chops recipe, and it's sure to be a smash-hit at your next round-up.

1/4	CUP DIJON MUSTARD
1/4	CUP HONEY
1	TABLESPOON ROASTED GARLIC (page 21)
	KOSHER SALT
3	TABLESPOONS ORANGE JUICE
1	TABLESPOON WORCESTERSHIRE SAUCE
1	TABLESPOON CHOPPED FRESH ROSEMARY LEAVES
12	4-OUNCE LAMB CHOPS

ORANGE-FIG-PECAN RELISH (makes 1 1/2 cups)

1/2	CUP WATER
1	CUP DRIED FIGS, TRIMMED AND CUT INTO SMALL PIECES
1	TABLESPOON GRATED ORANGE ZEST
1	CUP CHOPPED ORANGE SECTIONS (from 2 peeled oranges)
1	TABLESPOON HONEY
1	TEASPOON CHOPPED FRESH ROSEMARY LEAVES
1/2	CUP PECAN PIECES, TOASTED

In a long glass casserole dish, combine mustard, honey, garlic, salt, orange juice, Worcestershire sauce, and rosemary, mixing well. Add the lamb chops, turning in the mixture to coat well. Place dish in refrigerator to marinate for 30 minutes to 1 hour.

Prepare the grill. Remove the chops from marinade and cook over a hot fire for 3 to 4 minutes on each side. Serve with the orange-fig-pecan relish.

In a small pan, simmer the figs and zest, partially covered, for about 5 minutes, or until figs are tender and most of the water is gone. Transfer to a bowl and allow to cool. Stir in the orange, honey, and rosemary, and let stand for at least 30 minutes. Stir in the pecan pieces and serve with the lamb chops.

Cabrito Sage Sausage

Makes 3 pounds

If you have a Kitchen Aid stand-up mixer, use the grinder attachment. Otherwise, you should invest in the old-fashioned meat grinder that you attach to a kitchen counter. The effort is well worth the results, which is a rich sausage that makes an excellent taco filling, along with seasoned pinto beans. We like it also on hot biscuits with Green Chile–Cheese Grits on the side.

LOUIS LAMBERT

Recipes such as Grady's Cabrito Sage Sausage wouldn't be possible if not for his longtime pal Louis Lambert. Lou, who comes from a big ranching family in West Texas' Big Bend Region, was working for Wolfgang Puck at Postrio in San Francisco when Grady talked him into coming home to work with him at the Gage Hotel in Marathon. Lou then worked with Grady at Reata in Alpine and Fort Worth, and taught Grady loads of essential basics, such as the importance of always using fresh (never bottled) garlic and how to make great sausage. If you ever get to meet Lou, get him to tell you how he and Grady made a killer smoker out of an old refrigerator. To taste Lou's culinary genius, head to his Austin restaurant called Lambert's.

1¹/2	POUNDS BONELESS CABRITO, DICED
	(available at Mexican meat markets)
1¹/2	POUNDS BONELESS PORK BUTT, CHILLED AND DICED
2	TABLESPOONS SALT
1	TABLESPOON CRACKED PEPPER
1	TEASPOON GROUND CORIANDER
1	TEASPOON GROUND CUMIN
1	TABLESPOON MINCED GARLIC
1/4	CUP ROUGHLY CHOPPED SAGE
	PINCH OF CAYENNE PEPPER
1/4	CUP CHICKEN STOCK
	HOG CASINGS AS NEEDED (available at specialty meat markets)

Combine the meat and the spices on a sheet pan, mixing well by hand. Grind the meat and spices, using a medium die.

Mix the ground meat in a mixer fitted with a paddle attachment for 30 seconds on slow speed, adding the chicken stock while mixing. Mix for another 30 seconds, increasing to medium speed. Stuff the mixture into the casings, tying the casings at 4¹/2-inch intervals.

Refrigerate until ready to cook. To cook, grill over a hot fire or fry in a skillet over medium-high heat until the internal temperature reaches 140°F.

Pheasant–Sun Dried Tomato Sausage

Makes 3 pounds

This luscious sausage can be grilled and sliced on top of a Texas-style pizza, made with Guy Lee's Pan Del Campo (page 32) or cooked into a stew with corn, potatoes, and carrots, then served with a crusty bread and a cold Lone Star.

1	POUND PHEASANT MEAT, CHILLED AND DICED
1/2	POUND CHICKEN LEG MEAT, CHILLED AND DICED
1 1/2	POUNDS PORK BUTT, CHILLED AND DICED
2	TABLESPOONS SALT
2	TEASPOONS FINELY GROUND BLACK PEPPER
1	TEASPOON GROUND FENNEL SEED
1	BUNCH BASIL, ROUGHLY CHOPPED
1/2	CUP SUN-DRIED TOMATOES, DICED SMALL
1/2	CUP PARMESAN CHEESE, DICED SMALL
1/4	CUP CHICKEN STOCK
	HOG CASINGS AS NEEDED (available at specialty meat markets)

Mixing by hand, combine the meat, spices, and herbs. Grind meat mixture, using a medium die, until well combined. Transfer to a large bowl, add the sun-dried tomatoes and cheese, and mix for 30 seconds on slow speed, using a mixer fitted with a paddle attachment, adding the chicken stock slowly. Increase the speed to medium and mix for another 30 seconds.

Stuff the mixture into the casings, tying at 4 1/2-inch intervals. Grill over a hot fire or in a heavy skillet over medium-high heat until the internal temperature reaches 140°F.

5

THINGS YOU DON'T ROPE

MONOTONY WAS A CONDITION known all too well to the cowboy pushing cattle up what seemed like an endless trail. And while the coosie did his best with every edible available, cowboys must have been happy when the infrequent palate diversion came along. ✪ Few were prone to the chuck-wagon genius of the mystical Po Campo in Larry McMurtry's epic novel, *Lonesome Dove*. Po Campo persuaded a bunch of "meat 'n taters" cowboys to try his molasses-dipped fried grasshoppers, winning nearly all of them over with a prairie treat that tasted like candy. J. Frank Dobie wrote in *Cow People* about a beloved chuck-wagon cook who played a mean banjo and made a wonderful fried wild turkey. "A good cook left a good taste to linger long," Dobie wrote. "It belongs with memories of riders who stayed with the herd." ✪ Chicken has always been the obvious alternative to beef, but most bantams brought along for the drive were on hand to produce breakfast eggs. When cooks could find turkey, quail, dove, rabbit, squirrel, and rattlesnake, they became eats of the non-roping variety. And we can be fairly sure that the occasions to cross a river or stream were met with joy, assuming that a crafty coosie could snatch a few trout for the evening meal. ✪ In this chapter, we offer the best in Texas eats of the finned and feathered variety, including trout, red snapper, Gulf shrimp, oysters, and catfish, along with our extra-special chicken and dumplings recipe. Quail lovers will find an easy way to prepare this delicious Texas bird, too. ✪ As any cook can tell you, the key to creating excellent fish and chicken lies in putting the right treatments to work in your cooking to bring out the best in fish and poultry flavors and textures. We say that's done by finding great Texas produce, such as the huge and sweet Texas 1015 onions, juicy heirloom tomatoes, sweet corn, and Texas Ruby Red grapefruits, all found in recipes on the following pages. ✪ How those cowpokes would have loved extravagances like these.

Chicken-Fried Oysters with Pico Cream

PAGE 107
Cowboy Working with a Bronc in a Corral of the LS Ranch, Texas. 1907.

PREVIOUS SPREAD
Overlooking the Canadian River While Cowpunchers Put a Herd of LS Cattle Across It. 1907.

CHISHOLM TRAIL BIT

Although the famous trail was named for Indian trader Jesse Chisholm, there's a lot of confusion about others with same-sounding names from the period. In addition to the trail's namesake, there was Thorton Chisholm, no relation to Jesse, a Texas trail driver hailing from DeWitt County in the historic lands between San Antonio and Victoria. Thorton Chisholm is noted for having led an ambitious cattle drive to St. Joseph, Missouri.

Then there was John Chisum, a Texas cattleman who drove herds from Paris to Shreveport during the Civil War to supply the South with beef. At war's end, Chisum founded a ranch on the Concho River in West Texas. He eventually formed a partnership with the legendary Charles Goodnight and moved to New Mexico, where he became known as the Cattle King of the Pecos.

Makes 4 to 6 servings

Texas Gulf Coast oysters are a delicacy found in season most of the year, and our brand of frying them makes the plump mollusks even juicier. The rich, spicy sauce adds a little luxury to the down-home treat.

1 1/2	CUPS WHOLE MILK
2	DOZEN OYSTERS, SHUCKED
2	CUPS PEANUT OIL
2	EGGS, BEATEN
1	CUP BASIC SEASONED FLOUR (page 130)
	KOSHER SALT
3/4	CUP SOUR CREAM
3/4	CUP TEXAS PICO (page 156)

Pour 1 cup of the milk into a bowl and soak the oysters. Heat the oil in a large sauté pan over medium-high heat. While the oil is heating, combine the remaining 1/2 cup of milk and eggs in a separate bowl, mixing well. In still another bowl, combine flour and salt. Roll each oyster in seasoned flour, put into egg wash, and roll in flour mixture again. Fry in hot oil for 2 to 3 minutes on each side. Transfer to a paper towel–lined plate to drain.

To prepare the pico cream, place the sour cream and Texas pico in a blender and pulse just long enough to mix well. Chill the mixture about 20 to 30 minutes and serve with piping hot oysters for dipping.

Plank-Roasted Red Snapper with Citrus-Ancho Glaze

Makes 4 servings

Red snapper is another favorite catch from the Gulf of Mexico, and cooking it on a wooden plank gives extra flavor and aroma. Be sure to use clean, unvarnished hardwood such as cedar, hickory, maple, or oak, but avoid using pine. Brushing with this sweet-hot glaze, made even better with Texas Ruby Red grapefruit from the Rio Grande Valley, will boost flavor and keep the juiciness in, and your presentation on the wooden plank will definitely impress your dinner guests.

1	TEASPOON GRATED TEXAS RUBY RED GRAPEFRUIT RIND
2	TABLESPOONS TEXAS RUBY RED GRAPEFRUIT JUICE, FRESHLY SQUEEZED
2	TABLESPOONS HONEY
1	TABLESPOON FRESHLY GROUND ANCHO CHILE POWDER
1	TEASPOON GROUND CUMIN
1/2	TEASPOON GROUND CORIANDER
	KOSHER SALT
3/4	CUP (6-ounce can) THAWED ORANGE JUICE CONCENTRATE
2	TABLESPOONS PLUS 1 TEASPOON OLIVE OIL
4	8-OUNCE RED SNAPPER FILLETS
2	HARDWOOD PLANKS, MEASURING 12 BY 12 BY 1-INCHES
16	FRESH TEXAS RUBY RED GRAPEFRUIT WEDGES, PITH REMOVED
1/4	CUP FRESHLY CHOPPED CILANTRO

Combine the grapefruit rind, juice, honey, chile powder, cumin, coriander, salt, concentrate, and 1 teaspoon of the olive oil in a bowl and whisk until blended well. Brush the glaze onto both sides of the snapper fillets. Set aside.

Brush remaining olive oil onto the planks and place in a cold oven. Preheat the oven to 350°F for 15 minutes. Place the fish on the planks and bake for 15 minutes. Remove from the oven; turn the fish over, brush with glaze, and return to the oven for 5 minutes, or until the fish is sizzling crisp around the edges but just done in the center. Remove from the oven and serve hot, garnished with Ruby Red grapefruit sections and chopped cilantro.

Note: If not using wooden planks, bake the fish on a foil-lined baking sheet at 375°F for about 15 minutes.

Pan-Roasted Trout Ranchero

Makes 4 to 6 servings

Look all you want, but you can't find an easier fish recipe, nor one that delivers as much flavor with so little work. Unless, of course, you spend the weekend trying to hook the perfect trout. We recommend heading to your favorite fishmonger and asking him to fillet and butterfly the trout for you.

3	**TABLESPOONS OLIVE OIL**
4–6	**TROUT FILLETS, WITH SKIN, BUTTERFLIED**
	SEA SALT AND FRESHLY GROUND BLACK PEPPER
2	**TABLESPOONS BUTTER**
1	**1015 ONION (see page 217), PEELED, CUT IN HALF, AND SLICED INTO THIN, HALF-MOON RIBBONS**
4	**JALAPEÑOS, SEEDED AND CUT INTO MATCHSTICKS**
4	**CLOVES GARLIC, THINLY SLICED**
4	**ROMA TOMATOES, CUT IN HALF AND SEEDED**
	KOSHER SALT AND PEPPER
	JUICE OF 2 LIMES
	CILANTRO SPRIGS, JALAPEÑO SLICES, AND LIME WEDGES FOR GARNISH

Heat a large sauté pan over medium heat and add the olive oil. Season the trout with salt and pepper. Place the trout, opened and skin side down, in the pan. Cook for 1 to 2 minutes on each side, just until barely browning. Do not overcook. Place the trout on a platter and keep warm while you prepare the ranchero sauce. (You may have to cook the fish in two batches, depending on the size of the pan.)

In the same pan, heat the butter over medium-high heat and sauté the onion, jalapeño, and garlic for about 3 minutes. Add the tomatoes and sauté another 3 minutes, stirring well. Remove from heat and spoon the vegetables over the fish. Add salt and pepper to taste and drizzle with lime juice. Top with your favorite Cowboy Butter (page 143) and garnish with cilantro sprigs, jalapeño slices, and lime wedges.

Catfish Cakes with Chipotle Remoulade

Makes 6 to 8 servings

This spin on crab cakes puts to use the meaty, white fish that's plentiful in Texas lakes and throughout the South. Serve them as appetizers or add a salad and make these a meal, but just be sure to make the spicy Chipotle Remoulade sauce in advance to serve with the catfish cakes.

1/2	CUP BUTTER
1	MEDIUM WHITE ONION, FINELY CHOPPED
3	CELERY RIBS, FINELY CHOPPED
1	RED BELL PEPPER, STEM AND SEEDS REMOVED, FINELY CHOPPED
	KOSHER SALT AND PEPPER
2	TABLESPOONS PAPRIKA
2	POUNDS CATFISH FILLETS
1/4	CUP DIJON MUSTARD
3	EGGS, BEATEN
3	TABLESPOONS WORCESTERSHIRE SAUCE
1/2	CUP MAYONNAISE
2	CUPS DRY BREAD CRUMBS
1/2	CUP PEANUT OIL
1	CUP CHIPOTLE REMOULADE (page 157)

In a large skillet, melt the butter and sauté the onion, celery, and red bell pepper over medium heat until the vegetables just begin to soften. Season with salt, pepper, and paprika, and transfer to a bowl to cool.

Pat the catfish fillets dry with paper towels. Place the fillets in the bowl of a food processor and process until finely chopped. Transfer to a mixing bowl and combine with the mustard, eggs, and Worcestershire sauce. Add the cooled, sautéed vegetables and mayonnaise, and blend well. Gradually mix in 1 cup of the bread crumbs. Scoop the mixture into your hands and shape into thick cakes, adding bread crumbs as necessary to shape 6 to 8 cakes. Coat the cakes in more crumbs before frying.

In a deep skillet, heat 1/4 cup of peanut oil until hot and pan-fry the cakes for 2 minutes on each side over medium-high heat. Add oil as necessary. Serve with Chipotle Remoulade.

Frank Smith Watering His Horse, Cross-B Ranch, Crosby County, Texas. 1909.

Chiles Rellenos with Garlic Shrimp and Deviled Nuts

Makes 4 servings

One of our favorite traditional Mexican eats is a stuffed poblano chile, but believe it or not, this is one dish we think tastes better when it's not fried. The stuffing of sautéed garlic shrimp, fiery pecans, and lots of cheese makes this version extra special—and extra rich.

4	POBLANO CHILES
3	TABLESPOONS VEGETABLE OIL
1	WHITE ONION, FINELY CHOPPED
1	JALAPEÑO, SEEDED AND MINCED
2	MEDIUM TOMATOES, CHOPPED
8–10	CLOVES GARLIC, MINCED
1	POUND MEDIUM SHRIMP, PEELED, DEVEINED, AND COARSELY CHOPPED
1/2	CUP RED CHILE SAUCE (page 131)
1/2	CUP CHOPPED CILANTRO LEAVES
1	CUP DEVILED NUTS (page 153)
2	CUPS GRATED MONTEREY JACK CHEESE
1 1/2	CUPS TEXAS PICO (page 156)
1/2	CUP CRÈME FRAÎCHE (page 144)

Preheat the oven to 500°F. Place the poblano chiles on a lightly greased baking sheet and brush lightly on all sides with 1 tablespoon of vegetable oil. Place the sheet in the oven and allow the chiles to blister, turning until blackened on all sides. Remove from the oven and transfer chiles to a glass bowl. Cover with a dry dish towel and allow to cool. When the chiles are cooled, carefully slit open each one and remove the seeds and membrane. Set aside.

Heat the remaining 2 tablespoons of oil in a sauté pan over medium-high heat. Sauté the onion, jalapeño, tomatoes, and garlic for about 30 seconds, then add the shrimp, stir well, and sauté for 1 minute. Add the chile sauce and cook for another 1 minute, stirring occasionally. Remove from heat and cool. When the mixture is cool, add the cilantro, deviled nuts, and 1 cup of grated cheese, and mix well.

Adjust the oven temperature to 350°F. On a foil-lined baking sheet, place the roasted chiles, slit side up. Stuff each of the chiles with the shrimp mixture. Top with the remaining cheese and bake for 15 to 20 minutes, or until the mixture is thoroughly heated and the cheese is just beginning to brown on top. Serve with toppings of Texas Pico and crème fraîche.

Roasted Chicken with Tart Black Bean Salsa

Makes 4 servings

If you'll use thighs and legs when roasting chicken, you'll have juicier, more flavorful chicken every time. Brining the chicken also guarantees that you'll have a tender, moist chicken.

1/2	CUP PLUS 1 TABLESPOON KOSHER SALT
3	TABLESPOONS SUGAR
5	CUPS COLD WATER
4	CHICKEN LEG-AND-THIGH QUARTERS
1/2	CUP BUTTER, MELTED
1	TABLESPOON COARSELY GROUND BLACK PEPPER
1	TABLESPOON CHOPPED FRESH THYME
3	CLOVES GARLIC, MINCED
1	TABLESPOON DRIED MEXICAN OREGANO LEAVES
2	CUPS TART BLACK BEAN SALSA (page 119)
	FRESH CILANTRO SPRIGS, FOR GARNISH

To brine the chicken, combine 1/2 cup of the salt, sugar, and water in a large bowl and stir well until the salt and sugar dissolve. Place the chicken quarters in a large glass casserole dish and cover with the saltwater mixture. Cover with plastic wrap, place in the refrigerator, and allow to brine for 3 to 4 hours.

When ready to roast the brined chicken, preheat the oven to 425°F. Line a roasting pan with foil and lightly grease the pan's roasting rack. Place the chicken quarters on the rack. In a small bowl, combine the melted butter, the remaining 1 tablespoon of salt, pepper, thyme, garlic, and oregano. Brush the chicken with the butter mixture, reserving some of the mixture. Roast the chicken for about 25 minutes, basting midway through the cooking process with the remaining butter mixture. Finish roasting at 500°F for about 10 minutes to brown and crisp the exterior of the chicken. (Be sure to test the temperature at the fleshiest part of the chicken; you want the meat thermometer to read 180°F.) Serve each quarter atop 1/2 cup of Tart Black Bean Salsa and top with a sprig of fresh cilantro.

Tart Black Bean Salsa

Makes 6 to 8 cups

Using Granny Smith apples in the salsa adds a special crunch and a sweet-sour punch. It is also a good complement to Angele's Mudbug Mollies (page 68).

2	CUPS DRIED BLACK BEANS
16	CUPS WATER
2	LARGE EARS YELLOW CORN
1	TEASPOON VEGETABLE OIL
1	RED BELL PEPPER, STEM AND SEEDS REMOVED, CHOPPED INTO MEDIUM DICE
1	LARGE OR 2 SMALL GRANNY SMITH APPLES, CORED AND CHOPPED INTO SMALL DICE
1	CUP TEXAS PICO (page 156)
1	TEASPOON GROUND CUMIN
1	TEASPOON GROUND CHILE POWDER
2	TEASPOONS OLIVE OIL
1	TEASPOON WHITE VINEGAR

Place the black beans in a large bowl and cover with 8 cups of water. Let the beans soak overnight.

When you're ready to prepare the salsa, drain the black beans and cover with the remaining 8 cups of fresh water. Bring to a boil, then reduce heat to simmer. Cook the beans for about 2 hours, or until tender. Remove from heat, drain, and cool.

Meanwhile, preheat the oven to 450°F. Remove the husk and silks from the corn. Brush the vegetable oil on the corn and place on a baking sheet. Roast in the oven for 15 to 20 minutes, turning to roast evenly. Remove from the oven, cool, and cut corn from the cob.

In a medium-size bowl, combine the roasted corn, cooked black beans, and the remaining ingredients. Cover and set aside for 30 minutes. Serve chilled or at room temperature, but don't marinate too long or the vegetables will become soggy.

Old-Fashioned Chicken and Dumplings

Makes 6 to 8 servings

Lucky Texans are those who were raised by a mom or grandma with a mean pot of chicken and dumplings in her cooking artillery. This recipe might just be as good as those we grew up on; you'll find a little freshness lift from the addition of cilantro.

10	CUPS CHICKEN STOCK
6	CHICKEN THIGHS
6	CHICKEN LEGS
5	CUPS ALL-PURPOSE FLOUR
3	TABLESPOONS BAKING POWDER
2	TABLESPOONS KOSHER SALT
1	TABLESPOON FRESHLY GROUND BLACK PEPPER
2	CUPS HEAVY CREAM
2	TABLESPOONS MASHED ROASTED GARLIC CLOVES
1	LARGE ONION, DICED
6	LARGE CARROTS, DICED
	SALT AND PEPPER
1/4	CUP CHOPPED CILANTRO LEAVES

Heat the stock in a large, heavy pot and cook the chicken thighs and legs over medium-low heat for about 45 minutes to 1 hour, until very tender. Remove from heat and allow to cool, reserving the stock in its pot. Remove the chicken and discard the skin. Pick the chicken from the bones and set meat aside.

To make the dumplings, combine the flour, baking powder, salt, and pepper in a large mixing bowl and mix well. Add the heavy cream to mixture, stirring just until dough is thick and sticky. Turn onto a floured work surface and knead the dough until you can roll it out to a thickness of $1/16$ inch.

Add the garlic, onion, and carrots to the stock and reheat over medium heat just until boiling. Cut the dough into dumplings that measure 1 by 1-inch. Add the dumplings to boiling stock, cover, and simmer, cooking for about 20 minutes. Add the chicken meat and salt and pepper. Garnish with cilantro. Serve hot.

Chicken Breasts Stuffed with Chorizo and Fancy Cheeses

Makes 6 servings

Now this is the way to eat chicken breasts—stuffed with spicy Mexican sausage and lots of rich, creamy cheese, all basted in butter. This is a perfect dish to pair with Green Chile–Cheese Grits (page 45) or Spoonbread with Simple Chorizo (page 59).

3/4	CUP KOSHER SALT
5	TABLESPOONS SUGAR
7	CUPS COLD WATER
6	CHICKEN BREASTS, WITH SKIN AND BONE
2	POUNDS SIMPLE CHORIZO (page 101)
1	CUP GOAT CHEESE, CRUMBLED
1	CUP GRATED MONTEREY JACK CHEESE
	KOSHER SALT AND PEPPER
3	TABLESPOONS CHOPPED FRESH ROSEMARY
1	TABLESPOON CHOPPED FRESH THYME
4	TABLESPOONS BUTTER

To brine the chicken, combine the salt, sugar, and water in a large bowl and stir well until the salt and sugar dissolve. Place the chicken in a large glass casserole dish and cover with the water mixture. Cover with plastic wrap, place in refrigerator, and allow to brine for 3 to 4 hours.

When the brining is almost complete, prepare the stuffing by cooking sausage in a sauté pan over medium–high heat, until evenly browned. Drain the fat from chorizo immediately and transfer the chorizo to a bowl and allow to cool. When cooled, mix the chorizo with the cheeses, salt, pepper, and herbs. Set aside.

Place a chicken breast flat on cutting board or counter surface. Using a paring knife, cut a horizontal slit down the center of the fleshiest part of the breast, creating a pocket. Repeat with all the chicken breasts. Dividing the chorizo mixture evenly, stuff each of the chicken breast pockets.

Preheat the oven to 400°F. In a large sauté pan, melt 2 tablespoons of the butter. Cook the stuffed breasts, skin side down, over medium–high heat until browned. Transfer the breasts to a foil-lined baking sheet and bake for 30 minutes, or until chicken is thoroughly cooked. While the chicken is baking, melt the remaining 2 tablespoons of butter in a small sauté pan and use to baste the chicken breasts as they cook.

Cowboys of the Spur Ranch Putting the Herd Through a Gap in the Barbed Wire Fence. Spur Ranch, Texas. ca. 1908–1910.

Bob White Quail with Blue Ribbon Cornbread Patties

Makes 8 servings

Texas hunters bring in millions of bob white quail each fall, but most specialty butchers can provide you with these rich, meaty birds anytime. This easy recipe calls for a little spicy oil, a little rub, and a hot grill.

3/4	CUP BROWN SUGAR
2	TABLESPOONS KOSHER SALT
1	TABLESPOON FRESHLY GROUND BLACK PEPPER
1	TEASPOON PAPRIKA
3–4	TABLESPOONS RED CHILE OIL
16	SEMIBONELESS JUMBO QUAIL (rib and back bones removed but wings and legs intact)
2	CUPS CRUMBLED BLUE RIBBON CORNBREAD (page 168)
2	EGGS, BEATEN
1/2–3/4	CUP MILK
	KOSHER SALT AND FRESHLY GROUND PEPPER
	CRÈME FRAÎCHE (page 144)
1–2	FRESH JALAPEÑOS, SLICED

In a bowl, combine the brown sugar, salt, pepper, and paprika to make a rub. In another bowl, place the chile oil. Brush each of the quail with the chile oil, then coat completely in the rub. Set aside on a platter.

Preheat the oven to 425°F. In a large bowl, combine the crumbled cornbread, eggs, and enough milk just to moisten and make a fairly stiff dressing batter. Stir and season with salt and pepper. Using your hands, grab a fistful of the cornbread mixture and shape into patties, about 1/2 inch thick. Place the patties on a lightly greased baking sheet and bake for about 15 minutes, or until the patties are just browned. Remove from the oven and keep warm.

While the patties are baking, prepare a hot grill and cook the quail, turning once, until skin is well browned but the meat is still pink. Take care not to overcook. When the quail are done, place 1 to 2 cornbread patties on each plate and top with 2 quail. Drizzle with a little crème fraîche and garnish with sliced jalapeños.

6

FROM THE PANTRY AND LARDER

THE COOSIE'S KITCHEN was the campfire, of course, and the chuck wagon and chuck box served as his pantry and larder. But he was much more than a cook. Cowboys understood that the coosie ruled the camp. His power was not to be challenged. Only the trail boss was permitted exceptions. ✪ Between making meals that kept the drovers going, the coosie served as banker, barber, and even doctor. Besides meal provisions, he carried lamp oil, which could be used on minor injuries, Epsom salts, salves, liniments, and quinine in his chuck box. J. Frank Dobie wrote that the occasional coosie provided extras for the trail boss, such as fresh milk and eggs from a cow and bantam he'd bring along. ✪ The chuck wagon moved out early each day in search of the next night's camp, stopping when possible near water and wood. Before retiring at night, the coosie pointed the wagon's tongue toward the North Star to ensure that the drive would head in the right direction at daylight. The coosie carried firewood in a sling that resembled a hammock suspended from the wagon's underside. He burned dried cow chips in the absence of wood. Digging a trench in the dirt, the coosie started his fire in the afternoon. After cooking the evening meal, he cleaned up ever so quietly. The sudden clang of a skillet could startle the cattle and trigger a dreaded stampede. Then he retired for the night, and was up again at three in the morning, stoking the fire and preparing breakfast before the drive moved on. ✪ The bright spot in the cowboy's day was the evening meal, which infrequently included the unexpected wild onion in a stew or the surprise of sugar cookies. Though potatoes, flour, sugar, coffee, molasses, lard, and even dried apples were daily provisions, the discovery of berries, for instance, could boost a cowboy's spirits. ✪ In this chapter you'll find recipes for rubs, sauces, condiments, and butters that are indispensable for cooking our brand of cowboy fare. These are basics that show up in various dishes from chapter to chapter, so it's a good idea to keep the key ingredients on hand. They're simple to prepare, but they work to turn plain meals into flavor-packed memories.

Basic Seasoned Flour

Makes 2 cups

Our recipes for chicken-fried steak and onion rings call for this flour, but you can use it in any savory recipe calling for seasoned flour. Add extras such as paprika, cayenne, or dried oregano as you wish. Make a double batch and keep on hand in a jar.

2	CUPS ALL-PURPOSE FLOUR
1	TABLESPOON KOSHER SALT
1	TEASPOON FRESHLY GROUND BLACK PEPPER
1	TEASPOON FRESHLY GROUND WHITE PEPPER

Whisk all of the ingredients together in a bowl. Shake well before using.

PAGE 126
The Combined Outfits of the OR and Wagon Rod Interests in Roundup Camp, with the Remuda in the Distance. OR Range, Arizona. 1909.

PREVIOUS SPREAD
The JA Wagon Cook Taking a Shave, JA Ranch, Texas. Robert Faure ("Frenchy") Does the Shaving. 1908.

Red Chile Sauce

Makes 4 1/2 cups

When you let your imagination fly, you'll find that red chile sauce can be as versatile as tomato sauce. We use it in tamale fillings, venison chili, and enchilada sauces, but you'll find your own ways to incorporate it into recipes for meat loaf and hearty casseroles.

16	DRIED ANCHO CHILE PEPPERS, ABOUT 1/2 POUND
6	CUPS WATER
1/3	CUP WHITE WINE
1/2	WHITE ONION, PEELED AND DICED
5	CLOVES GARLIC, MINCED
5	TEASPOONS PACKED LIGHT BROWN SUGAR
2	TABLESPOONS GROUND CUMIN
2	TABLESPOONS HONEY
	KOSHER SALT AND FRESHLY GROUND PEPPER TO TASTE

Rinse the chiles to remove any dirt. Slit each chile with a sharp knife and remove and discard the seeds and stem. Wash your hands very well after this, as the peppers are hot. Wear gloves if you have sensitive skin. Place the peppers in a large saucepan and cover with water by 1 inch. Bring to a boil over high heat, then reduce the heat and simmer for about 15 minutes. The peppers should be soft and have absorbed some liquid. When cooked, remove the pan from the heat and set aside without draining.

While the peppers are cooking, combine the wine, onion, garlic, brown sugar, cumin, and honey in a small saucepan. Set this mixture over medium heat and simmer for about 10 minutes, or until the onions are soft. Remove from the heat and set aside.

Using tongs, transfer the cooled anchos to the container of a blender. Add about 2 cups of the ancho liquid and all of the onion broth. Cover the blender container and start blending at low speed, increasing to high speed as the puree becomes combined. The result will be a thick, dark red sauce. Adjust seasonings with salt, pepper, and more honey if desired. Use the sauce as is in a recipe, or place in a clean glass container and refrigerate. Use the sauce within a week or freeze for later use.

CATTLE DRIVING FACTS

• A steer worth $4 in Texas was worth $40 in Kansas or Missouri.

• The number of cattle driven from Texas rose dramatically: In 1867, 35,000 were driven north. In 1869, the number exploded to 600,000. The peak was 700,000 in 1879, with a decrease to 350,000 in 1873 and a drop-off to 166,000 in 1874 when a recession began. The number jumped again to almost 395,000 in 1880, but continued to slip after that.

• In addition to the Chisholm Trail, the Shawnee Trail, the Western Trail, and the Goodnight-Loving Trail were the better-known routes of the day.

• Drives from Texas usually began in the spring when cattle could feed on new grass as they moved north.

• A herd of steers could move about 10 to 15 miles a day, although some cowboys would push for 20 to 25 miles per day at the start to get the trail broken in.

• The daily drive typically would begin just after daybreak and breakfast, continue for four or five hours, and stop for "dinner," which is the old Texas term for the midday meal. The cattle would graze until about one in the afternoon, then be herded again until evening. The coosie moved ahead from breakfast to find the noon meal spot while the trail boss moved forward to find a place to bed down—preferably a spot with good grass and water—for the evening stop.

Roasted Green Chiles

Makes 1 cup

Our recipe for Green Chile–Cheese Grits (page 45) calls for these chiles, but you can use them on top of grilled chicken sandwiches or burgers, in enchilada recipes, and in omelets. Chopped, roasted chiles can be stored in an airtight container in the freezer for 1 month.

2–3	TEASPOONS VEGETABLE OIL
8–10	NEW MEXICO GREEN OR POBLANO CHILES

Preheat the oven to 500°F. Grease a large baking sheet or roasting pan with vegetable oil and arrange the chiles on sheet or pan. Roast the chiles in the oven, turning as necessary to blacken the chiles all over. When charred, remove from the oven and place in a large bowl. Cover completely with a towel and let the chiles cool for about 15 minutes. Slide the blackened skins off chiles, remove stems and seeds, and chop well.

Matador Trail Herd on the Move, Texas. 1910.

Piloncilla Rub

Makes 1 cup

Piloncilla is a Mexican brown sugar found in the produce section of Latin grocery stores and in many ethnic sections of grocery stores. Shaped into a hard cone, the sugar is easily grated down the cone sides with a serrated knife or a traditional grater. Used on our porterhouse pork chops, piloncilla also makes the base for a great rub on steak and chicken.

1   **CUP GRATED PILONCILLA**

1   **TABLESPOON KOSHER SALT**

1   **TABLESPOON FRESHLY GROUND CRACKED BLACK PEPPER**

In a bowl, combine all ingredients with a whisk until well mixed. Store in an airtight container at room temperature. Use brown sugar in place of piloncilla if necessary.

Caramelized Onions

Makes 1 ¹/₂ cups

Sweetened, deeply cooked onions make a rich addition to our Goat Cheese Mashed Potatoes (page 43). They're also great on grilled steak and burgers with blue cheese.

2	**TABLESPOONS VEGETABLE OIL**
1	**RED ONION, THINLY SLICED**
1	**WHITE ONION, THINLY SLICED**
1	**BUNCH GREEN ONIONS, CHOPPED**
3	**TABLESPOONS BALSAMIC VINEGAR**
1/4	**CUP BROWN SUGAR**

Heat the oil in a heavy sauté pan over high heat. Cook the onions, stirring constantly until softened, approximately 10 minutes. Add the vinegar and brown sugar, lower the heat, and simmer for 15 to 20 minutes, stirring occasionally, until the liquid is completely absorbed.

RED RIVER COUNTRY

The modern-day town of Bowie, Texas, lies near the old crossing points that were called Red River Station and Spanish Fort. Today, you'll find the Chisholm Trail Memorial Park that pays tribute to the period with a sculpture of nine Longhorns and two cowboys. In nearby Nocona, the town honors its trail days with a Chisholm Trail Ranch Rodeo at the Chisholm Trail Rodeo Arena.

Creamed Onion Jam

Makes 2 cups

Thicker in consistency than the Caramelized Onions on the previous page, this easy condiment goes on our Goat Cheese Sliders (page 27). Make it to spread on smoked ham or turkey sandwiches, as well as steaks. Serve cool or at room temperature.

2	TABLESPOONS VEGETABLE OIL
1	LARGE YELLOW ONION, THINLY SLICED
1	LARGE RED ONION, THINLY SLICED
2	BUNCHES GREEN ONION, COARSELY CHOPPED
3/4	CUP WHITE BALSAMIC VINEGAR
1/2	CUP BROWN SUGAR
1/2	TEASPOON GROUND MUSTARD
	KOSHER SALT
1	8-OUNCE PACKAGE CREAM CHEESE, ROOM TEMPERATURE

In a large skillet, heat the oil over medium heat. Add the onions and sauté until they start to soften and wilt. Add the vinegar, brown sugar, and mustard; lower the heat to a simmer and cook until the vinegar has been reduced by half. Stir in the salt and cream cheese, remove from heat, and cool. The jam can be stored in an airtight container in the refrigerator for one week.

Hollandaise Diablo

Makes 2 cups

This is easy to whip up in a blender, but you have to serve it immediately. And don't worry about these egg yolks; they're effectively cooked by the very warm butter and citrus acids. Try this atop fried oysters, beef tenderloin, or grilled salmon.

5	**LARGE EGG YOLKS**
1½	**CUPS BUTTER, MELTED AND VERY WARM**
	JUICE OF 2 LEMONS
2	**TEASPOONS TOMATO PASTE**
	HOT PEPPER SAUCE OR CAYENNE PEPPER
	KOSHER SALT

In a blender or food processor fitted with metal blade, pulse the egg yolks on low and slowly add the melted butter, lemon juice, tomato paste, hot pepper sauce, and salt. Serve over Chicken-Fried Oysters (page 110) immediately.

Two Cowboys Holding a Calf Down While a Third Applies the Hot Branding Iron, LS Ranch, Texas. 1907.

A lot of Grady's cowboy cooking is done over an open fire. Sometimes, the combination of a flame and Grady can be a little dangerous. Don't believe it? While we haven't been visited by the fire department yet, there have been some close calls.

Once Grady was cooking with his pal Park Kerr on Food TV's *Cooking Live with Sarah Molton* show. Park is the co-founder of the El Paso Chile Company and the author of several great cookbooks. Somehow in the process of making enchiladas and sipping margaritas, the paper on which the tortillas were drying managed to catch fire. On live television!

Another time he was teaching a cooking class in Granbury in a historic building just off the town square. He got a little too bois-terous when demonstrating one of his dishes, which he was cooking over a two-burner camp stove, and a fire erupted. Only briefly.

And then there was the Thanksgiving Day when the local NBC affiliate had him out to show how to deep-fry a turkey, a method that has been popular in Louisiana and has become a huge hit in Texas. It's an easy process, but you really have to watch your heat, which Grady didn't do very well. A fire broke out. The good news? The segment was being shot outdoors, and we put the fire out before we burned anything besides the turkey.

Oven-Dried Tomatoes

Makes about 3 cups

We use these tomatoes in tamale fillings as well as in our bread salad. You can use them in pasta sauces or with roasted red bell peppers and our red chile sauce to put on top of enchiladas.

12	ROMA OR PLUM TOMATOES
2	TABLESPOONS VEGETABLE OIL
2	TABLESPOONS CHOPPED FRESH THYME LEAVES

Preheat the oven to 250°F. Cut each tomato in half lengthwise. With a spoon, scoop out pulp and discard. In a bowl, toss the tomato hulls, oil, and thyme until the tomatoes are well coated. Place the tomatoes, skin side down, on a baking sheet, arranging so they are not touching.

Cook for about 1 1/2 hours, or until the tomatoes are dried. Remove from the oven and cool. Transfer to an airtight container and refrigerate.

Cilantro-Nut Mash

Makes 1 cup

Spread this rich concoction on your grilled fish or chicken or add to freshly cooked rice to make a great side dish for lamb chops. By removing the cilantro from the recipe, you'll have a simpler nut mash to use in the Buttermilk and Nut-Mash Biscuits (page 162).

1	CUP CHOPPED FRESH CILANTRO LEAVES
1/4	CUP (1 ounce) GRATED PARMESAN CHEESE
1/2	CUP CHOPPED PECANS
2	CLOVES GARLIC, MINCED
1/4	CUP OLIVE OIL
2	TABLESPOONS SMOOTH GOAT CHEESE
	KOSHER SALT

Combine the cilantro, cheese, pecans, and garlic in a food processor. Process by pulsing and gradually adding the oil. Add the goat cheese and season with salt, processing just until slightly smooth.

Cowboy Butters

Makes 8 to 10 servings

These flavored butters create a luxurious effect when put atop a sizzling steak, fresh from the grill. Experiment with various additions to the butter for use on your favorite grilled meats and poultry, too, as well as on baked potatoes and breads and in grits.

BANDERA BUTTER

1	CUP UNSALTED BUTTER, SOFTENED (not melted)
1/4	CUP CHOPPED CILANTRO LEAVES
1	TABLESPOON KOSHER SALT
3	CLOVES GARLIC, MINCED
5	OVEN-DRIED TOMATOES, CHOPPED (page 140)

Using a food processor, blend all ingredients just until smooth. On a sheet of parchment or waxed paper, shape the butter into a log that measures about 1 1/2 inches wide. As you roll the butter into a cylinder, be sure to remove any air pockets. Wrap the paper tightly around the log, secure with freezer tape, and place in the freezer one hour before serving. Slice the disks of butter onto steaks at serving time. The logs will store up to one month in freezer.

GREEN BUTTER

1	CUP UNSALTED BUTTER, SOFTENED (not melted)
2	CUPS COARSELY CHOPPED, LOOSELY PACKED CILANTRO LEAVES
1/2	CUP COARSELY CHOPPED GREEN ONIONS
	KOSHER SALT

Process the ingredients just until smooth. Follow the directions for Bandera butter above.

ROASTED GARLIC BUTTER

2	TABLESPOONS ROASTED GARLIC (page 21)
1	CUP UNSALTED BUTTER, SOFTENED (not melted)
	KOSHER SALT
1	TEASPOON GROUND WHITE PEPPER

Puree the roasted garlic in food processor. Add the butter and process until light and fluffy. Season with salt and white pepper to taste and follow the directions for Bandera butter.

RED CHILE BUTTER

1	CUP UNSALTED BUTTER, SOFTENED (not melted)
4	TEASPOONS FRESHLY GROUND ANCHO CHILES OR CAYENNE PEPPERS
1/2	TEASPOON GROUND CUMIN
	KOSHER SALT

Process the ingredients until light and fluffy. Follow the directions for Bandera butter.

TRAIL DRIVE GLOSSARY

Chuck-wagon A wagon that carried food, supplies, and cooking equipment on a trail drive.

Cow Pony A tamed horse.

Drag Rider A cowboy who rides at the rear of the herd to keep it moving.

Dutch Oven A large, covered pot that was heated from the bottom and the top.

Flank Rider A cowboy who rides at the side of the herd to keep it from spreading out.

Point Rider A cowboy who rides at the front of the herd on a trail drive.

Remuda Extra horses taken on the drive.

Roundup The act of collecting and sorting cattle for a trail drive.

Stampede An event in which startled cattle suddenly run in all directions.

Swing Rider A cowboy who rides alongside a herd to turn it in the right direction.

Trail Boss The cowboy in charge of all other cowboys and cattle on the drive.

Wrangler The cowboy in charge of the remuda on the trail.

Source: Texas Historical Commission

Crème Fraîche

Makes 2 1/4 cups

You'll quickly see that this very simple addition puts a little flair on dishes, such as Frito Pie (page 28) and Pinto Bean Chowder (page 52). Use it just like you would sour cream, but be sure to make it ahead.

2   CUPS WHIPPING CREAM

4   TABLESPOONS BUTTERMILK

     KOSHER SALT

Combine the cream and buttermilk in a glass bowl. Cover and let stand in refrigerator for 8 to 24 hours, or until thick. Stir well and refrigerate for up to 10 days.

Barbecue Sauce

Makes 1 1/2 cups

In Central Texas, barbecue sauce tends to be the thinner, tart kind; while in North Texas, it's a thicker and a little sweeter. Our version has a little bite to it, but you can adjust the seasonings to suit your taste. Use this in our grilled quail recipes and on your own grilled chicken and beef dishes.

1	CUP WHITE BALSAMIC VINEGAR
1/2	CUP TOMATO PUREE
2	TEASPOONS GROUND CUMIN
2	TEASPOONS GROUND BLACK PEPPER
2	TEASPOONS GARLIC POWDER
1	TEASPOON GROUND MUSTARD
1/4	CUP BROWN SUGAR
	KOSHER SALT

In a medium-size bowl, combine all ingredients and whisk until well blended. Cover and set aside for 1 hour before serving. Store refrigerated, in an airtight container, for up to 2 weeks.

Jose Falcón's Slaw

Makes 2 cups

Anyone who has traveled in Texas's Big Bend area and taken the little boats across the Rio Grande to Boquillas has probably eaten Jose's incredible tacos. This is a version of his slaw, which makes a great addition to our Pushcart Taquitos (page 26) and tostadas.

1	CUP THINLY SHREDDED RED CABBAGE
1/2	CUP THINLY SHREDDED GREEN CABBAGE
1	RED BELL PEPPER, CUT INTO VERY THIN STRIPS
1	BUNCH CILANTRO LEAVES, CHOPPED
1/4	CUP MAYONNAISE
3	TABLESPOONS MALT VINEGAR
2	TEASPOONS SUGAR

Toss the shredded cabbage, red bell pepper, and cilantro in a large bowl, mixing well. In a small bowl, whisk together the mayonnaise, vinegar, and sugar until sugar is dissolved. Pour the mixture over the cabbage mixture and toss well to coat. Cover and refrigerate for 1 hour before serving.

Charley Thompson (left) and Ed Bomar Having a Game of Seven-up, Turkey Track Ranch, Texas. 1906.

CHISHOLM TRAIL BIT

A herd of three thousand cattle required a team of ten to fifteen cowboys, including the trail boss, wrangler, and coosie. The cowboys worked in pairs. The top hands were the pointers, those who rode at the head of the herd as guides. The swing riders rode about one third of the way back, followed by the flank riders, and the drag riders rode at the back, the dustiest and least desirable position.

Smoky Caesar Salad Dressing

Makes 6 to 8 servings

Here's a deeper, bolder version of a favorite. We've taken the classic recipe and added just a hint of chipotle to give it a tiny boost.

4	EGG YOLKS
2	ANCHOVY FILLETS
1	TEASPOON WORCESTERSHIRE SAUCE
1	TEASPOON DIJON MUSTARD
2	CLOVES GARLIC, MINCED
	JUICE OF 1 LEMON
2	TEASPOONS WHITE WINE VINEGAR
	FRESHLY GROUND BLACK PEPPER
1	TEASPOON BOTTLED CHIPOTLE SAUCE
1 1/2	CUP OLIVE OIL

In the bowl of a food processor, combine all ingredients except the olive oil. Process until pearly and smooth. With the processor running, add olive oil in a slow, steady stream and process for 1 to 2 minutes to thicken. Serve immediately or chill slightly before serving.

Caesar Croutons

Makes 2 cups

Use these on our Caesar Salad with Barbecued Quail (page 39), or on any green salad topped with grilled beef or chicken. You'll need about six day-old biscuits to make this recipe.

1/4	CUP OLIVE OIL
2	TABLESPOONS MINCED GARLIC
2	TABLESPOONS CHOPPED FRESH ROSEMARY
	KOSHER SALT
2	CUPS DAY-OLD BUTTERMILK AND NUT-MASH BISCUITS
	(page 162), CUT INTO 3/4-INCH CUBES

Preheat the oven to 375°F. In a bowl, combine the olive oil, garlic, rosemary, and salt. Toss the biscuit cubes in a large bowl with the oil mixture to coat. Spread the cubes onto a baking sheet and bake for 20 to 25 minutes, or until golden brown. Cool and add to salad.

Bread-and-Butter Jalapeños

Makes about 3 quarts

If you like bread-and-butter pickles, these will get your taste buds going. Make plenty to keep in the icebox, where they'll keep fine for a month. Use them on burgers, grilled chicken sandwiches, with pork roast, or in pulled brisket tacos.

3/4	POUND FRESH JALAPEÑOS, ABOUT 20–30
1	CARROT, PEELED AND COARSELY CHOPPED
1	RED ONION, THINLY SLICED
20	CLOVES GARLIC, PEELED
1	TEASPOON DRIED THYME LEAVES OR 3 (3-inch) SPRIGS FRESH THYME, CHOPPED
4	CUPS APPLE CIDER VINEGAR
4	CUPS LIGHT BROWN SUGAR
1/4	CUP EXTRA-VIRGIN OLIVE OIL
1	TABLESPOON KOSHER SALT

Select a large glass jar about 3 quarts to 1 gallon in size. Wash it well and rinse with boiling water to sterilize. Pour the water out. Set the jar aside.

Wash the peppers and make sure they are clean, especially at the stem end. Dry thoroughly. Pack the peppers, carrots, onion, garlic, and thyme into the jar, mixing or shaking to distribute the vegetables evenly.

Heat the vinegar in a large nonreactive saucepan to just boiling. Remove from heat and stir in the brown sugar and olive oil. Stir well until the sugar has dissolved. Return mixture to heat if necessary to help dissolve the sugar. Pour the hot liquid over the peppers and stir again. Place a small plate over the peppers if necessary, to keep them submerged. Set the peppers aside to cool. When cool, cover tightly and place the jar in the refrigerator for at least one day before serving.

Jalapeño-Apple Jelly

Makes 6 eight-ounce jars

You'll always be tempted to serve this fiery jelly on lamb chops, but don't overlook pork chops and pork tenderloin. Spread it on turkey sandwiches during Thanksgiving weekend, or pile it on our buttermilk biscuits.

8	**GRANNY SMITH APPLES, PEELED, CORED, AND DICED** (about 8 cups)
3	**CUPS WATER**
1	**CUP CIDER VINEGAR**
6	**JALAPEÑOS, STEMS AND SEEDS REMOVED, DICED**
3	**CUPS SUGAR**
1	**6-OUNCE BOTTLE LIQUID FRUIT PECTIN**

Place the apples, water, vinegar, and jalapeños in a large, heavy saucepan. Bring to a boil over medium-high heat, stirring occasionally. As soon as the mixture boils, lower the heat to medium and cook for about 20 minutes, or until the apples soften. Remove the pan from heat. Using a fine-mesh strainer, strain the liquid into a clean large, heavy saucepan, letting the apples drain, but do not press on them. When the liquid is extracted, discard the pulp. Add the sugar to the apple juice and bring to a boil over medium-high heat. Remove from heat, add pectin, and stir well. Pour into 6 sterilized jars, seal, and store.

THE TRAIL MUSEUM

The entire story of the famous trail is told in glorious detail at the Chisholm Trail Heritage Center in Duncan, Oklahoma. Inside, you'll learn the background of the 1,200-mile trail and the cowboys who worked it, along with the reaction of the Indians to this experience of man and beast. Outside, you can't help but be impressed with the magnificent bronze sculpture, measuring 16 feet by 35 feet, of a chuck wagon followed by Longhorn cattle, cowboys, and a trail dog.

Deviled Nuts

Makes 4 cups

Use your favorite chile powder to make these peppy nuts, which go well on salads and in our chiles rellenos. Be sure to experiment with cashews, almonds, and peanuts, as all make great holiday gifts.

4	**CUPS** (about 1 pound) **PECAN HALVES**
1/2	**CUP UNSALTED BUTTER, MELTED**
4	**TEASPOONS FRESHLY GROUND CHILE POWDER**
1/2	**CUP PACKED BROWN SUGAR**

Preheat the oven to 350°F. In a large bowl, toss the pecans in the melted butter until they are completely coated. Sprinkle the chile powder over the nuts and toss them until coated completely. Add the sugar and toss them with your hands to keep the sugar from forming lumps. Spread the mixture onto a lightly oiled baking sheet, scraping the residue from the bowl on top of the nuts. Bake for 20 minutes, or until the nuts begin to brown and the butter begins to spread. At this point, the coating won't be crunchy, but as the nuts cool, the coating will harden. These nuts can be stored in an airtight container until needed for up to two weeks.

All-Around Beef Rub

Makes 1 1/2 cups

This might be the best flavor-enhancer for steaks, pork, and chicken you'll ever make. Keep plenty of this dry rub on hand, and be sure to add paprika, cumin, cayenne, or other ground red chiles as you like.

1/4	CUP KOSHER SALT
1	CUP BROWN SUGAR
1/4	CUP COARSELY GROUND BLACK PEPPER

In a bowl combine all of the ingredients, blending well. Store at room temperature in an airtight container. Make sure to remix the seasoning before each use.

A JA Chuck Wagon in Full Operation, JA Ranch, Texas. 1908.

Texas Pico

Makes 2 cups

Our version of pico de gallo is an indispensable condiment. It's a key ingredient to our Frito Pie (page 28), but you'll find that it's perfect on tacos, fish, and baked potatoes, too. Dress it up with diced avocado to add a little richness.

6	JALAPEÑOS, SLICED
1	RED ONION, DICED
6	GREEN ONIONS, THINLY SLICED
2	TOMATOES, DICED
2	BUNCHES CILANTRO LEAVES, STEMS REMOVED AND MINCED
	JUICE OF 2 LIMES
	KOSHER SALT

Toss the jalapeños, onions, tomatoes, and cilantro in a bowl. Drizzle with lime juice and top with salt, and toss again to combine. Let sit for about 15 minutes before serving.

Chipotle Remoulade

Makes 2 cups

Our Mexican-inspired version of a classic Creole sauce is fabulous on any kind of fish, from our hot catfish cakes and fried oysters to grilled snapper and freshly boiled shrimp. You'll be hooked in no time.

1/2	CUP FINELY CHOPPED CELERY
1/2	CUP CHOPPED WHITE ONION
4	TABLESPOONS WHITE VINEGAR
4	TABLESPOONS FRESHLY SQUEEZED LIME JUICE
2	TEASPOONS KOSHER SALT
1	TEASPOON FRESHLY GROUND PEPPER
4	TABLESPOONS SPICY BROWN OR CREOLE MUSTARD
1–2	CANNED CHIPOTLE CHILES
1	TABLESPOON SAUCE FROM CANNED CHIPOTLE CHILES
1	CUP VEGETABLE OIL

In a blender or the bowl of a food processor, combine all ingredients except the vegetable oil. Pulse several times until the ingredients are just chopped. On low to medium speed, slowly add the oil until the sauce is well blended and thickening. Cover and refrigerate for 1 to 2 hours before serving.

7

FROM THE BAKERY

COWPOKES DIDN'T LIVE BY BREAD ALONE, but only the foolish would assume the cowboy would willingly go a day without eating something baked. That's pretty much been true for most civilizations throughout time, and it hasn't changed today. ✪ Soon after guests are seated at the Chisholm Club, a basket of our buttermilk biscuits are served with some Texas Port Jelly—all of which disappears quickly. That goes to show that Texans always have and always will love biscuits, and not just for breakfast. The version we include here incorporates a nut mash for more texture, which you'll find makes a fine accompaniment to chicken-fried steak and rich mashed potatoes. They're every bit as good with pinto bean chowder or spinach salad topped with fancy cheeses. ✪ A chuck-wagon meal has never been complete without a batch of biscuits cooked over a fire in a Dutch oven. You can bake them in the oven that way, of course, just as you can a batch of the butter-rich Blue Ribbon Cornbread found in this chapter. For a sweeter, more Southern-style cornbread, you'll want to fry up a batch of Mary Lou's Hot-Water Cornbread, a popular soulfood mainstay and a legacy from the longtime, dearly loved proprietress at the Nutt House in Granbury. ✪ Your breakfasts have never been more delicious than with our Butterscotch Rolls, Cranberry-Peach Bread and Sourdough Flapjacks with Cowboy Blueberry Butter. Those flapjacks, of course, can be served with anything from jalapeño-apple to Texas Port Jelly, but we think you should try flapjacks in other ways, too. They're fine with savory additions of chorizo, roasted chicken, and the tender meat pulled from our Braised Pig Trotters and Beef Short Ribs. ✪ Bread is one of the great staples in comfort food and should always be regarded as a pleasure and a treat. Ours come from old recipes that would make your grandma proud and a trail-worn cowboy feel like a brand-new man.

Buttermilk and Nut-Mash Biscuits

Makes 10 large biscuits

Be sure to make twice as many of these as you think you'll need, because they tend to get eaten up in a big hurry. We serve them at Grady's restaurants with our Texas Port Jelly (page 164), but they're pretty darn good just by themselves.

2	**CUPS ALL-PURPOSE FLOUR**
1	**TABLESPOON SUGAR**
2	**TEASPOONS BAKING POWDER**
1	**TEASPOON KOSHER SALT**
1/4	**TEASPOON BAKING SODA**
1/4	**CUP SOLID VEGETABLE SHORTENING**
1/4	**CUP (4 tablespoons) UNSALTED BUTTER, CHILLED**
1/2	**CUP CILANTRO-NUT MASH (page 141)**
3/4	**CUP BUTTERMILK**
2	**TABLESPOONS MELTED BUTTER OR OLIVE OIL**

Preheat the oven to 450°F. Place the flour in a large bowl. Add the sugar, baking powder, salt, and baking soda. Blend with a fork or a whisk. Add the shortening and the unsalted butter. Cut the shortening and butter into the dry ingredients with a pastry blender or two forks until the mixture resembles fine crumbs. The fat should be evenly distributed in the flour. Fold in the cilantro-nut mash with a spatula. Add the buttermilk and gently mix by hand until everything is just moistened and the dough forms a ball.

Turn the dough out onto a lightly floured surface and knead three or four times. Do not overwork the dough, or the biscuits will not be tender. Roll or press the dough into a slab about 1/2 inch thick. Cut biscuits using a 3-inch cutter dipped in flour to prevent sticking. Place the biscuits about 1 inch apart on an ungreased sheet pan. Let the biscuits sit at room temperature to rise a bit more before baking, about 10 minutes. Place the biscuits in the oven and bake for 10 to 12 minutes, or until golden brown. Remove the biscuits from the oven and brush with melted butter while still hot. Serve warm.

PAGE 158
Sam Whittaker, Wagon Cook for the LS, Getting Breakfast in the Early Dawn, LS Ranch, Texas. 1907.

PREVIOUS SPREAD
The Matador Wagon Cook [Harry Stewart] Making a Cobbler. Matador Ranch, Texas. 1908.

Texas Port Jelly

Makes 3 eight-ounce jars

A good port makes a great jelly, as diners have found out when dining with Grady. This is a favorite, served with our buttermilk biscuits, but it's also good with pork chops and roasted chicken.

2	CUPS PORT
3	CUPS SUGAR
1	TABLESPOON LIME JUICE
2	CINNAMON STICKS
3	OUNCES LIQUID FRUIT PECTIN

Combine the port, sugar, lime juice, and cinnamon sticks in a large, heavy saucepan and bring to a boil. Boil for 2 minutes, stirring, and remove from heat. Add the pectin, mixing well. Cool the mixture and transfer to three sterilized jars, seal, and store.

The Chuck Wagon Is Out and Three Block Cowpunchers, Jim Finch, J. F. Weissienger and Lord Taylor (Wagon Boss), are Eating a Meal, Three Block Ranch, New Mexico. 1908–1909.

CHISHOLM TRAIL BIT

"Traditional cook crankiness was based on duty and a desire to keep camp in order. Beyond a radius of about sixty feet—the length of the longest roping rope—from the wagon his power ended. No man was supposed to ride up close enough or fast enough to scatter dust over pot, pan, food, or fire. Only the boss could hitch his horse to a wagon wheel. No man could walk in and take a snack, even a cup of coffee, unless given permission, until the cook announced "chuck" breakfasting was less uniform. No matter how friendly he might be with the hands, the cook, like an army officer, found avoidance of familiarity helpful to authority. A servitor, he nevertheless dominated. Before the wagon moved, every cowboy was expected to tie up his bedroll and put it in the wagon bed. If he left it on the ground, an accommodating cook might roll it up and carry it; a tough one might leave it behind. Let the owner ride back, pack it in—and learn a lesson."

Cow People, J. Frank Dobie, 1964

Mary Lou's Hot-Water Cornbread

Makes 8 to 10 servings

Mary Lou Watkins made the Nutt House Restaurant in Granbury, Texas, famous long before Grady had the good fortune to run the same eatery. Folks drove from all over to eat her food, particularly her hot-water cornbread. These little cornbread patties are just slightly sweet, and they're fried, rather than baked, in a cast-iron skillet.

1	CUP WHITE CORNMEAL
1	CUP YELLOW CORNMEAL
2	TEASPOONS SALT
1	TABLESPOON SUGAR
2	CUPS BOILING WATER
2–3	TABLESPOONS BACON DRIPPINGS
1/2	TEASPOON BAKING POWDER
2	TABLESPOONS COLD WATER
1	CUP VEGETABLE OIL

In a large, heavy bowl, mix the cornmeals, salt, and sugar. Stir in the boiling water and drippings and blend well. Cool the batter for 15 to 20 minutes. Stir the baking powder into the cold water to dissolve, then add to the batter and mix well. In a deep skillet, heat the oil to 380°F for frying. While the oil is heating, make small cornbread patties with your hands, shaping them a little less than 2 inches in diameter. Fry in hot oil just until golden brown, turning once. Drain on a paper towel-lined plate and serve with a Cowboy Butter (page 143) or Texas Port Jelly (page 164).

Blue Ribbon Cornbread

Makes 8 to 10 servings

Several years ago, June took home a first-place ribbon at the State Fair of Texas for her cornbread, which has become a family favorite. Use this recipe to make cornbread patties, which go well with grilled Bob-White Quail (page 124). It will also make a darn good stuffing, too.

1/2	CUP BUTTER
1	CUP YELLOW CORNMEAL
1	CUP ALL-PURPOSE FLOUR
1	TABLESPOON BAKING POWDER
1/2	TEASPOON SALT
3/4	CUP HEAVY CREAM
1	EGG, BEATEN
1/2	CUP CHOPPED RED BELL PEPPER
3/4	CUP GRATED SHARP CHEDDAR CHEESE
1–2	JALAPEÑOS, STEMS AND SEEDS REMOVED, MINCED

Preheat the oven to 425°F. Place butter in a 9 to 10-inch cast-iron skillet or Dutch oven and place in oven for 5 to 10 minutes, or until butter has melted. Remove from oven, and carefully tilt pan to make the butter coat the entire inside. Set aside.

In a large bowl, combine the cornmeal, flour, baking powder, and salt, and mix together with a whisk or fork. Make a well in the center of the dry ingredients and add the cream, egg, and red bell pepper. Pour the melted butter from the skillet into the mixture and mix with a whisk just until all ingredients are moistened. Spoon one-half of the batter into the skillet. Carefully spread the cheese over the batter and top with the minced jalapeños. Top with the remaining batter and bake for 20 to 25 minutes, or until the cornbread is just browning on top. Cool for 10 minutes before slicing and serving.

Butterscotch Rolls

Makes 15 to 18 rolls

There's never been a better breakfast treat than these old-fashioned sweet rolls. Bake up a big batch and serve them with smoked bacon, a platter of your favorite eggs, and a serving of Green Chile–Cheese Grits (page 45), and you'll be set at least until suppertime.

DOUGH

3/4	CUP MILK
1/2	CUP BUTTER
1/2	CUP SUGAR
2	TEASPOONS SALT
2	1/4-OUNCE PACKAGES DRY ACTIVE YEAST
1/2	CUP WARM WATER
1	EGG
4	CUPS ALL-PURPOSE FLOUR

TOPPING

1/4	CUP CORN SYRUP
1	TABLESPOON WATER
2	TABLESPOONS BUTTER, PLUS 1/4 CUP MELTED BUTTER
1	CUP BUTTERSCOTCH BITS
1	CUP CHOPPED PECANS
2/3	CUP FIRMLY PACKED BROWN SUGAR

Prepare the dough by bringing milk just to a simmer in a large saucepan. Stir in the butter, sugar, and salt. Remove from heat and cool until lukewarm. In a large bowl that you've warmed with hot water (but dried thoroughly), dissolve the yeast in warm water. Stir in the lukewarm milk mixture, egg, and half of the flour. Beat until smooth. Stir in the remaining flour to make a stiff dough. Cover tightly with foil and refrigerate for at least eight hours and up to 24 hours. When ready to form the rolls, remove the dough from refrigerator while you make the topping.

Preheat the oven to 350°F. Prepare the topping by combining the corn syrup, water, and the 2 tablespoons of butter. Bring to a boil, stirring constantly. Remove from the heat and stir in the butterscotch bits until they melt. Spread the mixture in a greased 9 by 13-inch baking pan and sprinkle with the pecans. Divide the chilled dough in half. Roll each half into a 9 by 12-inch rectangle. Brush each rectangle with the melted butter and sprinkle each half with brown sugar. Roll up tightly, starting from one of the 9-inch sides. Cut each roll into nine 1-inch slices. Place the slices in the pan about an inch apart on top of the butterscotch mixture. Cover and allow to rise in a warm area until doubled in size, about 1 hour. Bake the rolls on the middle rack for 20 to 25 minutes, until golden brown. Invert the rolls on a plate and serve warm.

Sourdough Flapjacks with Cowboy Blueberry Butter

Makes 12 six-inch pancakes

Once you've made flapjacks (the cowboy's most special breakfast) with sourdough, you'll have a hard time making any other pancake again. The addition of sourdough starter makes the pancakes melt-in-your-mouth light. Top these flapjacks with our Cowboy Blueberry Butter.

1/2	CUP BUCK'S SOURDOUGH STARTER (page 87)
2	CUPS ALL-PURPOSE FLOUR
2	TEASPOONS BAKING SODA
1	TABLESPOON SUGAR
1/2	TEASPOON SEA SALT
2	TEASPOONS GROUND CINNAMON
1/2	TEASPOON GROUND NUTMEG
2	EGGS, BEATEN
2	CUPS BUTTERMILK
1/4	CUP VEGETABLE OIL
1/2	TEASPOON VANILLA EXTRACT

Before preparing your flapjacks, let the portion of sourdough starter sit at room temperature overnight. At cooking time, heat up your griddle. In a medium-size bowl, sift the dry ingredients together and set aside. In another bowl, combine the eggs, buttermilk, oil, and vanilla with the starter. Carefully add the dry to the wet ingredients, stirring just until blended. Cook on a greased griddle over medium-high heat.

COWBOY BLUEBERRY BUTTER

1	CUP UNSALTED BUTTER, SOFTENED (not melted)
1/2	CUP FRESH BLUEBERRIES, RINSED (if frozen, thaw and drain well)

Using a food processor, blend the butter and blueberries just until smooth. On a sheet of parchment or waxed paper, shape the butter into a log that measures about 1 1/2 inches wide. As you roll the butter into a cylinder, be sure to remove any air pockets. Wrap the paper tightly around the log, secure with freezer tape, and place in freezer one hour before serving. Slice the disks of butter onto flapjacks at serving time. The logs will store up to one month in freezer.

Chocolate-Zucchini Muffins

Makes 12 muffins

We discovered these little gems in our travels around Texas. Great with an afternoon cup of coffee, these muffins are also a perfect brunch item when your menu includes a molasses-glazed ham.

1 3/4	CUP ALL-PURPOSE FLOUR
2	TEASPOONS BAKING SODA
1	TABLESPOON GROUND CINNAMON
1	TEASPOON GROUND NUTMEG
1/4	TEASPOON GROUND CLOVES
1/2	TEASPOON SALT
1/2	CUP COCOA POWDER
1/2	CUP GRANULATED SUGAR
3/4	CUP LIGHT BROWN SUGAR
4	EGGS, BEATEN
3/4	CUP BUTTERMILK
1/2	CUP VEGETABLE OIL
2	CUPS GRATED, PARTIALLY PEELED ZUCCHINI
3/4	CUP CHOPPED PECANS

Preheat the oven to 350°F. In a large bowl, combine the flour, baking soda, cinnamon, nutmeg, cloves, salt, and cocoa powder. Mix with a whisk to blend evenly. In a separate bowl, combine the sugars with the eggs, buttermilk, and oil, and mix well. Stir in the grated zucchini. Make a well in the center of the dry ingredients and slowly, carefully add wet ingredients to the center, mixing well with a whisk just enough to moisten. Do not overmix. Fold in the pecans. Spoon the batter into the wells of a greased muffin pan. Bake for 30 to 40 minutes, or until a wooden pick inserted in the center of a muffin comes out clean. Cool pan on a wire rack for 10 to 15 minutes before removing the muffins from the pan.

Flanking a Calf at Branding Time. Two Cowpunchers Are Ready to Hold It Down for the Branding, One Flips Him High off the Ground. Spur Ranch, Texas. 1901-1910.

COWBOY POETRY

What's become of the punchers
We rode with long ago?
The hundreds and hundreds
 of cowboys
We all of us used to know.

*Traditional, attributed to
N. Howard Thorp, ca. 1910*

Cranberry-Peach Bread

Makes 1 nine-inch loaf

Parker County peaches from the farmers' market in Weatherford (that's old cattle-driving country, of course) are hard to beat in summer and are the key to this delicious bread. Spread some cinnamon-laced cream cheese on top for a sinful snack, or slice it, slather it with butter, and heat it on a griddle for breakfast.

1	CUP ALL-PURPOSE FLOUR
1	TABLESPOON BAKING POWDER
1/2	TEASPOON SALT
1	TEASPOON GROUND CINNAMON
1/2	TEASPOON GROUND NUTMEG
1	CUP WHOLE WHEAT FLOUR
1/3	CUP PACKED BROWN SUGAR
1/2	CUP CHOPPED PECANS
1/2	CUP MASHED FRESH PEACHES (if canned, drain well)
1	CUP BUTTERMILK
1/4	CUP VEGETABLE OIL
1	EGG, BEATEN
1	TEASPOON PEACH OR VANILLA EXTRACT
1	12-OUNCE PACKAGE FRESH CRANBERRIES

Preheat the oven to 375°F. Sift the flour, baking powder, salt, cinnamon, and nutmeg into a large bowl. Add the whole wheat flour, brown sugar, and pecans, and mix well. Make a well in the center of the mixture and set aside. In another bowl, combine the peaches, buttermilk, oil, egg, and extract and mix well. Add to the dry mixture, stirring just enough to moisten ingredients. Carefully fold in the cranberries. Spoon the mixture into a greased Bundt or loaf pan and bake for 45 to 55 minutes, or until a tester inserted into the middle comes out clean. Cool the pan on a wire rack for 15 minutes. Remove from the pan and serve warm with softened cream cheese, if you like.

8

BEFORE THE BEDROLL

ANYONE WITH ROOTS reaching deeply into Texas soil probably grew up eating the handheld dessert known as the fried pie. A lasting legacy from the cattle-drive days, this primitive delicacy was made by chuck-wagon cooks who would prepare them for cowboys—if they were living right. Flour, lard, and sugar were items easily and always carried in the chuck box, and the pie could be fried up in a skillet without much trouble. As best as we can tell, cowboys loved the rare days that they were treated to apricot fried pies, which were preferable to the more readily available variety made from dried apples. Even today, you'll notice that apricot is the gold standard for fried pies. ✪ Texans continue to hold these treats in the same high esteem we do other ultimate-comfort delights, such as the Frito pie and chicken-fried steak. But unless you're willing to find places like Shirley's Burnt Biscuit Bakery in the West Texas town of Marathon, you can't find many traditional fried pies anymore. Better learn how to make them, we say, using Shirley's recipe in this chapter. ✪ Here, you'll also find two more of Grady's great passions, the butterscotch pie and Dutch-oven cobbler, which are probably as old as Texas, too. Sweet bliss also awaits in the East Texas blackberry crisp and the buttermilk pie, two treasures with a Southern accent that happen to be favorites from June's family. Be sure when baking those pies you incorporate our Cowboy Pie Crust, which gets extra flavor from a scattering of cinnamon. ✪ This chapter calls for plenty of dairy products, as you'll soon see. Buttermilk is needed if you're planning to make the buttermilk pie, buttermilk ice cream, and Dutch oven cobbler. Stock up on heavy cream if your sights are set on making Burnt Caramel Custard, East Texas Blackberry Crisp, and Cajeta Ice Cream Sandwiches. Don't forget the butter, too, one of Grady's favorite ingredients. ✪ Today's cowboys don't have to settle for bacon-grease pies or a baked bread concoction called Dirty George. If they're lucky, they'll go to bed with sweet dreams of Grandma Spears's Dr Pepper Cake, as will you.

Butterscotch Pie with Cinnamon Whipped Cream

Makes 1 pie or 8 to 10 servings

Your search for wonderful, homemade butterscotch pie could be as long as a West Texas drought. Good thing we've got a jewel of one right here. Top it with cinnamon-laced whipped cream and chopped pecans, and you'll be in heaven.

1	COWBOY PIECRUST (page 185)
1	CUP PACKED LIGHT BROWN SUGAR
2	TABLESPOONS ALL-PURPOSE FLOUR
2	CUPS COLD MILK
2	TABLESPOONS UNSALTED BUTTER
2	EGG YOLKS
1	TEASPOON PURE VANILLA EXTRACT
	PINCH OF SALT
3	TEASPOONS GROUND CINNAMON
2	CUPS WHIPPED CREAM
2	TABLESPOONS FINELY CHOPPED PECANS

Prepare the pie shell and chill in the refrigerator while making the filling. Preheat the oven to 350°F. Combine the brown sugar and flour in a medium saucepan, with a whisk. Gradually add the milk, continuing to blend. Set the pan over medium heat and continue to stir with a wooden spoon until the mixture has thickened. Remove from heat and add the butter, egg yolks, vanilla, and salt, stirring well. Gently pour the mixture into the pie shell. Set the pie on a baking sheet and bake for about 40 minutes, or until the pie is set. A knife inserted into the center will come out moist but clean when the pie is cooked; note that filling will seem very jiggly but will firm up when completely cooled. Remove the pie and place it on a rack to cool, or chill it overnight in the refrigerator. At serving time, fold the cinnamon into the whipped cream and use it to garnish the pie slices. Top with a scattering of finely chopped pecans.

Grandma Spears's Dr Pepper Cake

Makes one 9 by 13-inch sheet cake or a 3-layer, 8-inch cake

Grady's great-grandmother actually made a Coca-Cola cake, but Dr Pepper is just so much more Texan. You can bake this super-rich cake in a single layer pan for a sheet cake, or get fancy and make it a three-layer creation.

CAKE

1	CUP BUTTER
1	CUP DR PEPPER
3	TABLESPOONS COCOA
1/2	CUP BUTTERMILK
1	TEASPOON BAKING SODA
1	TEASPOON VANILLA EXTRACT
2	EGGS
2	CUPS ALL-PURPOSE FLOUR
2	CUPS SUGAR

FROSTING

1	CUP BUTTER
3	TABLESPOONS COCOA
6	TABLESPOONS DR PEPPER
1 1/2	CUPS SIFTED CONFECTIONERS' SUGAR

Preheat the oven to 350°F. Prepare the cake: In a saucepan, heat the butter, Dr Pepper, and cocoa until boiling. Remove from the heat and let cool. In a mixing bowl, combine the buttermilk, baking soda, vanilla, and eggs, mixing well. In a separate bowl, combine the flour and sugar. Combine all three mixtures until blended. Pour the batter into a greased 9 by 13 by 2-inch pan. Bake for 20 to 25 minutes, or until done. Test by inserting a toothpick at center of cake; if free of crumbs, it's done.

While the cake is baking, prepare the frosting by combining the butter, cocoa, and Dr Pepper in a saucepan; bring to a simmer. Whisk in the sugar and remove from heat. Cool slightly before spreading on the cake as described below.

When the cake is done, remove from the oven and pierce holes throughout the cake with a wooden skewer. Spread the frosting on the cake and let cool.

Mary Lou's Buttermilk Pie

Makes 1 pie or 8 to 10 servings

Mary Lou Watkins, the longtime matriarch of the Nutt House Restaurant in Granbury, became legendary for her version of this classic. Eat this at room temperature, or heat it and serve ice cream on top. You can make what's known in Texas as rancher's pie by adding ½ cup shredded coconut and ½ cup drained, crushed canned pineapple to the batter.

1	COWBOY PIECRUST (page 185)
2	CUPS SUGAR
2	TABLESPOONS CORNMEAL
5	EGGS, BEATEN
2/3	CUP BUTTERMILK
2	TABLESPOONS MELTED BUTTER, ROOM TEMPERATURE
1	TEASPOON VANILLA EXTRACT
2	TEASPOONS MINCED LEMON RIND
3	TEASPOONS LEMON JUICE

Preheat the oven to 350°F. In a bowl, combine the sugar and cornmeal. Add the eggs and buttermilk, mixing well. Add the butter, vanilla, lemon rind, and lemon juice, and mix until blended. Pour into the pie shell and bake for 45 minutes, or until just beginning to brown on top.

Cowboy Piecrust

Makes 1 nine-inch pie crust

West Texas baking maven Shirley Rooney makes the best piecrust in the world. She says the trick is in working the dough until it's as soft and smooth "as a baby's bottom." Be sure to level your measurements for the dry ingredients: no guessing allowed.

1 1/3	CUPS PLUS 1 TO 2 TABLESPOONS ALL-PURPOSE FLOUR
1/2	TEASPOON SALT
1/2	TEASPOON GROUND CINNAMON
1/2	TEASPOON SUGAR
1/2	CUP VEGETABLE SHORTENING, CHILLED
3	TABLESPOONS COLD WATER

Mix the flour, salt, cinnamon, and sugar in a medium-size bowl. Cut in the vegetable shortening, using a pastry blender or two knives, until all the flour is blended in and the mixture consists of pea-size bits. Sprinkle the mixture with water, 1 tablespoon at a time. Toss lightly with a fork until the dough forms a ball. Work the dough, pressing between your hands to form a 5- to 6-inch pancake. If dough seems too sticky, wrap in plastic and refrigerate for 20 to 30 minutes.

Dust the dough lightly with the 1 or 2 extra tablespoons of flour. Roll the dough in a circle between two sheets of waxed paper on a slightly dampened countertop. Peel off the top sheet of waxed paper, then trim the dough so that it has about 1 inch lapping over the edges of the 9-inch pie plate. Turn the dough over onto the pie plate, pull the waxed paper away, and press the pastry to fit the pan. Fold the edge of the pastry under and flute the edges or press with fork tines. Add desired filling and bake.

WILDCAT PIE

1/2 pound suet
1 cup water
1/2 cup vinegar
Flour as needed
1 cup sugar
Pastry dough
Dried peaches (optional)

Chop the suet and fry out. Discard the crackling. Add the water and bring to a boil. Add the vinegar. Stir flour in slowly, creaming to form a paste. Add the sugar and pour into a dough-lined pie tin. Cover with dough. Cut numerous openings for steam to escape, sprinkle sugar over the top, and bake until the crust is crisp and brown. The result tastes surprisingly similar to a fruit pie.

Cow Country Cookbook, by Dan Cushman (1992, Clear Light Publishers, Santa Fe)

East Texas Blackberry Crisp

Makes 8 to 10 servings

Nothing's better in summer than picking fresh blackberries alongside an East Texas lake and cooking up an old-fashioned crisp. It's easy and sure to be a hit with family and friends. Don't forget the Buttermilk Ice Cream (page 193).

CRISP

2	POUNDS BLACKBERRIES
	(substitute frozen when fresh are not available)
1	CUP HEAVY CREAM
1¹/2	CUPS SUGAR
1/4	CUP ALL-PURPOSE FLOUR
3	TABLESPOONS GROUND CINNAMON
	JUICE OF 2 LIMES
1	TEASPOON SALT

TOPPING

1¹/2	CUPS ALL-PURPOSE FLOUR
1	CUP BROWN SUGAR
1	CUP COLD UNSALTED BUTTER, CUT INTO ¹/4-INCH PIECES

Preheat the oven to 350°F. Prepare the crisp by combining the ingredients in a large bowl. Pour the mixture into a greased casserole dish.

Prepare the topping by combining the flour and brown sugar, mixing well. Cut in the butter using your hands to mix until well combined. Crumble the topping over the blackberry mixture, making sure to cover the surface of the top. Bake for 45 minutes to 1 hour, or until the topping is set. Serve warm or at room temperature.

Burnt Caramel Custard

Makes 6 servings

In fancier places, they call this *crème brûlée*, but that seems a little pretentious in a cowboy's cookbook. The important thing is that it's rich and a little sweet, and we figure it's what's for dessert in heaven. Experiment with your own version, substituting almond liqueur or Kahlúa for the vanilla extract, or adding a few fresh raspberries.

COWBOY VERSE

"SUNDOWN IN
THE COW CAMP"

Ol' Charlie's got his guitar out;
That Charlie sure can play. And
it's sundown in the cow camp—
It's my favorite time of day.

Some cowboys turn in early—
The cook's the first to go—
While the night owls hug the
    coffee pot
Till the fire's a dull red glow.

That strong and silent cowboy
type—The one you read about—
He's kinda forced to be that way
When the drive's all scattered out.

But he'll get downright eloquent
When the evening chuck's
    washed down,
And it's sunset in the cow camp,
With the crew gathered 'round.

Joel Nelson
New Cowboy Poetry: A
Contemporary Gathering, (1990)

8	**EGG YOLKS**
1/3	**CUP SUGAR**
2	**CUPS HEAVY CREAM**
1	**TABLESPOON VANILLA EXTRACT**
1/4	**CUP LIGHT BROWN SUGAR**

Preheat the oven to 300°F. Put six ramekins (or glass custard cups, about 4 to 6 ounces in size) in a large roasting pan and set aside. In a large bowl, whisk together the egg yolks and sugar until the sugar dissolves and the mixture becomes thickened and light yellow in color. Add the cream and vanilla, and continue to whisk until mixed well. Strain into a large bowl, skimming off bubbles and foam.

Divide the mixture evenly among the ramekins. Pour very hot water into the roasting pan, filling it until the water comes halfway up the sides of the ramekins. Bake until the custard is set around the edges, 50 minutes to 1 hour. Remove from the oven and leave in the water until it cools. Remove cups from the water bath and chill for 2 to 3 hours. At serving time, sprinkle 2 teaspoons of brown sugar over each custard. Use a small, handheld torch to brown the sugar or place the cups under a hot broiler until the sugar starts to crackle and turn dark brown. Return to the refrigerator and chill for about 5 minutes before serving.

Dutch-Oven Strawberry Cobbler

Makes 8 servings

Here's another great use for your Dutch oven. If you don't have one, a favorite casserole dish or deep baking pan will do fine. Just be sure to use fresh, ripe strawberries for the best flavor.

FILLING

4	CUPS SLICED FRESH-HULLED STRAWBERRIES
1	CUP SUGAR
3	TABLESPOONS FLOUR
1 1/2	CUPS WATER
1	TABLESPOON LEMON JUICE
2	TABLESPOONS BUTTER, MELTED
	PASTRY (recipe follows)
1	TABLESPOON GROUND CINNAMON

PASTRY

1 3/4	CUPS ALL-PURPOSE FLOUR
2	TABLESPOONS SUGAR
2	TEASPOONS BAKING POWDER
1	TEASPOON SALT
1/4	CUP SHORTENING, COLD
6	TABLESPOONS HEAVY OR WHIPPING CREAM
6	TABLESPOONS BUTTERMILK
3	TABLESPOONS BUTTER, MELTED

Preheat the oven to 350°F. Place the strawberries in a lightly greased Dutch oven. Make the syrup by combining 3/4 cup of the sugar and flour in a bowl; add the water and lemon juice, mixing well. Pour the syrup over the berries; bake for about 15 minutes while preparing the pastry.

Adjust the oven temperature to 425°F. Prepare the pastry by combining the flour, sugar, baking powder, and salt. Cut in the shortening, a little at a time, until the mixture resembles coarse crumbs; stir in the whipping cream and buttermilk. Knead the dough four or five times; roll to about 1/4-inch thickness on a lightly floured surface. Cut the dough to fit baking dish. Place the pastry over the hot berries; brush with melted butter. Bake at 425°F for 20 to 30 minutes, or until the pastry is golden brown. Before serving, combine the remaining 1/4 cup of sugar and the cinnamon, and sprinkle over the hot cobbler. Serve with buttermilk ice cream.

Cajeta Ice-Cream Sandwiches

Makes 6 to 10 sandwiches

Cajeta is a thick, syrupy combination of goat's milk and brown sugar. Here, we use it to fashion a Mexican-flavored ice cream that might be your favorite new taste. This cajeta ice cream makes a great companion to our cobbler and crisp, and it's a special treat when you put it inside these cookies.

ICE CREAM

2	CUPS CANNED GOAT'S MILK
2	CUPS HEAVY CREAM
8	EGG YOLKS
1 1/3	CUPS BROWN SUGAR
	PINCH OF KOSHER SALT

Bring the goat's milk and cream to a boil, then remove from heat. In a steel bowl, whisk the egg yolks with the sugar and salt, and gradually whisk in the hot cream and milk. Return to the saucepan and cook over low heat until the mixture thickens, about 10 minutes. Strain into a chilled bowl set in an ice-water bath and chill until cooled thoroughly. Freeze in an ice-cream maker according to machine instructions. When frozen but still soft, spread onto half the cookies to make sandwiches.

SANDWICH COOKIES

3/4	CUP BUTTER, ROOM TEMPERATURE
1/2	CUP SUGAR
1	EGG YOLK
1	VANILLA BEAN, SEEDS REMOVED
1 1/4	CUPS ALL-PURPOSE FLOUR
1/4	CUP COCOA POWDER
	KOSHER SALT
10	OUNCES WHITE CHOCOLATE, GRATED OR FINELY CHOPPED

Combine the butter and sugar until smooth. Beat in the egg yolk and vanilla until dough forms. Add the flour, cocoa, and salt, beating between each addition. Roll out between sheets of waxed paper and chill in refrigerator for 2 to 4 hours. Preheat the oven to 300°F and line a baking sheet with parchment paper. Cut the dough into rounds or rectangles, place on the lined baking sheet, and bake for 20 minutes. Remove to wire racks to cool. Meanwhile, melt the white chocolate in a double boiler. Dip the cooled cookies into chocolate. Let dry on wire racks. Spread ice cream on the cookies, top with cookies, and place in the freezer until firm.

Buttermilk Ice Cream

Makes 6 cups

As long as you're taking the time to crank out some homemade ice cream, do it right by using buttermilk. The flavor is much richer and more satisfying.

1	CUP WATER
1	CUP SUGAR
2	CUPS BUTTERMILK
	JUICE OF 1 LIME
1	TABLESPOON CORN SYRUP
	PINCH OF KOSHER SALT
1	TEASPOON LIME ZEST, GRATED

In a saucepan, combine the water and sugar, and bring to a boil. Remove from heat and refrigerate until chilled. Add the buttermilk, lime juice, corn syrup, salt, and zest. Freeze in an ice-cream maker according to machine instructions.

Shirley Rooney's Apricot Fried Pies

Makes 4 to 6 pies

Cowboys and ranch folk will drive from all over West Texas for just one of Shirley's phenomenal fried pies. Apple are good, but apricot are the best. Shirley's doors open at 6:15 in the morning, and we're here to tell you, these pies make a dandy breakfast.

FILLING

1	**POUND DRIED APRICOTS** (preferably California apricots)
4	**CUPS WATER**
1/2	**CUP SUGAR**
1/2	**TEASPOON GROUND CINNAMON**
1/4	**TEASPOON GROUND CLOVES**

PASTRY

2 1/2	**CUPS ALL-PURPOSE FLOUR**
1/2	**TEASPOON SALT**
2	**TABLESPOONS SUGAR** (optional)
3/4	**CUP SHORTENING**
6–7	**TABLESPOONS COLD WATER**

Prepare the filling by covering the dried apricots with water in a saucepan and cooking slowly, simmering for about 1 hour, until soft. Mash well with a potato masher and add the sugar, cinnamon, and cloves. Set aside to cool.

Prepare the pastry by sifting together the flour, salt, and sugar. Cut in the shortening with a pastry blender or two knives. Combine lightly until this mixture resembles cornmeal or tiny peas. Sprinkle water over the flour mixture, a tablespoon at a time, and mix lightly with a fork, using only enough water so that the pastry will hold together when pressed gently into a ball. Roll out dough to $1/8$ inch to $1/4$ inch in thickness. Using the bottom of a coffee can, cut the dough into rounds and place about 3 to 4 tablespoons of the filling on one half of each round. Moisten edges of dough with water, and pull the uncovered half of the round over the filling and press together to seal. Use fork tines or your fingers to crimp edges of the dough. (Note: Use a 6-inch mold or cutter with scalloped edge if you have one.)

You can place the pies on a lightly greased baking sheet and bake at 400°F for about 30 minutes or until the crust is golden brown, or you can deep-fry them in a skillet in oil heated to 350°F.

9

CAMPFIRE COCKTAILS

J. FRANK DOBIE AND OTHER WRITERS who detailed the lives of cattle drovers agree that cowboys weren't permitted to drink while with the herd. A drunk cowboy was a tremendous liability when the job was to move thousands of valuable livestock up a long road for months at a time. So it stands to reason that once those cowboys hit a town for rest and relaxation, their first stop was a saloon. There, they'd find heaven in letting off some steam over shots of whiskey, games of cards, and the companionship of warm, willing women. ✪ Cowpokes and greenhorns feel pretty much the same way today; we like to unwind at the end of a long day over drinks with friends and family. We like it even better when the choices and flavors in libations are as enjoyable as the day was challenging. ✪ The Kentucky Club Margarita found in this chapter is the same recipe used when the cocktail was created at that very bar in Juarez in 1942. Like several drinks we've included, it should be made using a shaker and strained into cocktail glasses, which can be either the vintage champagne glass or the classic martini glass. Of course, the modern-day margarita glass is always acceptable. ✪ You'll find plenty to enjoy in Janie's Sangria, a foolproof party favorite made for years by June's mom, and one that can be made with either red or white wine and plenty of fresh fruit. Fruit lovers will also enjoy the Will Rogers Cooler, La Paloma, the Brazos River Rambler, and the Stonewall Slush, which all call for fresh Texas fruit. ✪ Be sure to always use premium liquors in making these cocktails. People who say you can use a cheap brand and not taste the difference are lying, because the good stuff always shines through. In the same vein, be sure to use freshly ground coffee when making our Nuevo Laredo Coffee. Just be happy you don't have to use a hand-cranked grinder like the camp cooks did at the chuck wagon. ✪ Also, remember to thank your lucky stars that we have so many fine wines and cocktails today. Those trail cowboys had some pretty rough whiskey to drink, along with primitive chokecherry wine. And always remember, don't drink and drive cattle—or anything else.

Janie's Sangria

Makes 6 to 8 servings

Nobody whips up a meaner batch of sangria than June's mama, Janie. She uses whatever fresh fruits are available for flavoring the wine and for making the perfect drink to go with spicy dishes. During the summer, you can use white wine instead of red wine, and add lemon thyme to the batch.

2	BOTTLES DRY RED WINE
2	ORANGES, SLICED
2	LEMONS, SLICED
2	LIMES, SLICED
2	CUPS RED GRAPES
2	PEACHES, PITTED, PEELED, AND SLICED
2	APPLES, CORED AND SLICED
1	BOTTLE CHAMPAGNE (or club soda)
	ICE

The day before serving, pour the wine in a large container and add half of the sliced oranges, lemons, limes, and grapes and all of the peaches and apples. Cover and chill in the refrigerator. At serving time, remove the fruit and add champagne, and garnish with the reserved fresh grapes and fresh slices of orange, lemon, and lime. Pour over glasses of ice and enjoy.

The Texas wine business is by no means new, but the growth explosion over the past few years might lead you to think so. Fact is, Val Verde Winery in Del Rio was established in 1883 by Italian immigrants and is operated by the fourth generation of family winemakers today.

By 2002, more than 45 wineries were in business in Texas. One of the newer upstarts is the Chisholm Trail Winery in Fredericksburg, a town that has long known success in the vineyard business thanks to excellent wines produced nearby in Stonewall at Becker Vineyards. The Texas Wine and Grape Growers Association likes to point out that although production and winemaking styles vary, the wineries are linked together by a common "pioneer spirit which has persevered."

There are seven wine trails throughout the state for winery touring. In North Texas, the Munson Trail includes La Buena Vida and Delaney, among other Grapevine wineries. The Southeast Texas has the Brazos Trail, home to Messina Hof in Bryan. The Balcones Trail and Enchanted Trail in Central Texas include Dry Comal Creek and Becker Vineyards, respectively. The Highland Trail in the Hill Country includes Fall Creek Vineyards, and West Texas is home to the Pecos Trail, with Ste. Genevieve Wines, and the Palo Duro Trail, with the famous Llano Estacado.

Lupecola

Makes 2 servings

One of Grady's all-time favorite cooks, Lupe Sanchez, swears by this concoction. Trust us, Lupe knows what tastes good. You can substitute the juice from two limes for the Rose's, if you like.

	ICE
3	OUNCES PRESIDENTE BRANDY
	DASH OF ROSE'S LIME JUICE, ABOUT 10 DROPS
	COCA-COLA TO FILL THE SHAKER
	LIME WEDGES, FOR GARNISH

Fill the cocktail shaker three-quarters full with ice cubes. Add the brandy, lime juice, and Coca-Cola. Cover and shake well. Strain the drink into chilled cocktail glasses and serve. Garnish with the lime.

Tarleton Dr Pepper

Makes 2 servings

They still make Dr Pepper with pure cane sugar down in the town of Dublin, near Stephenville. We don't know if it's true that Tarleton State University students in Stephenville use DP as a mixer, but we thought this came close to making the right spiked Texas flavor.

ICE

4   OUNCES AMARETTO DI SARONNO

DR PEPPER TO FILL THE GLASSES

Put the ice cubes into highball glasses. Pour the Amaretto and Dr Pepper into the glasses, stir well, and serve.

Kentucky Club Margarita

Makes 2 servings

Among several versions regarding the creation of Texas's favorite cocktail is the one claiming it was invented in 1942 in Juárez by a bartender named Francisco Morales. Today you'll get the perfect margarita made in the same bar, the Kentucky Club, by Lorenzo Hernandez. Lorenzo has been in the same spot just across the international bridge on Avenida Juárez for more than fifty years. Lorenzo uses real Mexican limes. You should, too. You'll taste the difference.

JUICE OF 4 MEXICAN LIMES

1/4 CUP KOSHER SALT

2 OUNCES SILVER TEQUILA (Herradura is excellent)

2 OUNCES COINTREAU

ICE

Moisten the rims of the cocktail glasses with lime juice and invert in a saucer of salt. Shake the tequila, Cointreau, lime juice, and ice together in a shaker and strain into the glasses.

Stonewall Slush

Makes 2 servings

Some of Texas's most delicious peaches come from Gillespie County, and in summer you'll see fruit stands piled high with these beauties around the town of Stonewall. This refreshing, icy drink will set you right on a hot summer day.

It was a warm, spring day in 1866 when the first large herd of Texas Longhorns lumbered into Fort Worth on the way to beef-hungry markets in the north. Texas was flush with the wily, cantankerous critters. The herds had been abandoned during the Civil War as able-bodied men rode off to fight, and the Longhorns proliferated on the open range. Millions were there for the gathering.

Colonel J. J. Meyers led that first herd to Fort Worth. He and his cowhands and wagons started in Lockhart, near Austin, and were headed for Sedalia, Missouri. His herd of Longhorns represented the beginning of the great cattle drives that would come with increasing frequency through Fort Worth to railheads in Kansas and Missouri. From 1867 to 1872, an estimated 3 million head of cattle were driven up the Chisholm Trail from Texas.

Art Chapman,
Fort Worth Star-Telegram

2	CUPS SLICED PEACHES, FROZEN
1	CUP SLICED STRAWBERRIES, FROZEN
1 1/2	CUPS WHITE GRAPE JUICE
	STRAWBERRIES AND RED GRAPES, FOR GARNISH

In a blender, combine the peaches and strawberries with the white grape juice. Blend for 30 seconds, stopping once to stir the ingredients. Pour into tall glasses and garnish with the strawberries and grapes.

Jen's Favorite

Makes 2 servings

Necessity continues to be the mother of invention, as we found out one evening when A&W cream soda was the only mixer available. Paired with vodka, it makes a sweet, after-dinner belly warmer, and the addition of vanilla beans gives it a little panache. You can vary the garnish by substituting a cinnamon stick or a few freshly roasted coffee beans for the vanilla beans.

ICE

3 OUNCES VODKA

CREAM SODA TO FILL THE GLASSES

2 VANILLA BEANS

Fill cocktail or Collins glasses with the ice cubes. Pour the vodka into the glasses and top off with the cream soda. Garnish with vanilla beans.

Nuevo Laredo Coffee

Makes 2 servings

Two tasty Mexican libations go into this drink, guaranteed to
warm up any cowboy who's spent a long, cold day on the trail.

2	CUPS HOT COFFEE, FRESHLY BREWED
1	TEASPOON SUGAR
1½	OUNCES KAHLÚA
1½	OUNCES TEQUILA
	WHIPPED CREAM
	GROUND CINNAMON

Pour the coffee into two mugs and dissolve the sugar
in it immediately. Divide the Kahlúa and tequila between
the mugs, stirring well. Top with the whipped cream
and sprinkles of cinnamon.

PAGE 196
*Tom King, Matador Cowboy,
Drinking from the Brim of His Hat
at a Spring in Dutchman Pasture,
Matador Ranch, Texas. 1905.*

PAGE 199
*Matador Cowboys Celebrating at the
Lubbock, Texas, Railroad Yard after
Delivering a Shipment of Cattle. 1910.*

*Settling the Dust [LS Cowboys
Drinking at a Bar], Old Tascosa,
Texas. 1907.*

Just a few years ago, Grady was invited to cook on Rosie O'Donnell's talk show in New York. To make it a pure cowboy setting, he shipped Rosie a custom-made cowboy hat, along with a load of western accoutrements, including boots, hay bales, and ropes. And, of course, he sent some calf fries.

Rosie—wearing her new hat from Fort Worth—helped make the seasoned flour and the batter for the chicken-fried steak. Admitting she'd never heard of sourdough starter, she slugged on the beer that was used in the batter and fell a little behind in pounding her top round steak. Grady told her she'd never make it working in a Texas café.

While the chicken-fried steaks cooked, Grady offered Rosie a calf fry, explaining that "it's a calf testicle, a mountain oyster." Horrified, she yelled at him, "There's no need for that, Grady!" She questioned whether such things were really eaten, and he assured her they are, collected in a bucket during roundup time. She wanted no part of it.

Finally, Grady challenged Rosie to a roping contest. If she won, he'd eat a whole plate of calf fries. Neither won the roping challenge, and she refused to try a fry. If Grady meets her again, he'll try to talk her into some of his chicken-fried foie gras, served at the Chisholm Club.

La Paloma

Makes 2 servings

Translated as "the dove," this Mexican cocktail is perfect for those who like the citrus tang of the margarita rather than the sweetness. Add a fresh sprig of mint if you like.

3 OUNCES TEQUILA

JUICE OF 1 LIME

8 OUNCES FRESH GRAPEFRUIT JUICE

ICE

SPRIG OF MINT

Combine all of the ingredients in a shaker, shake well, and strain into cocktail glasses.

Brazos River Rambler

Makes 2 servings

The Chisholm Trail crossed the Brazos River at what's known today as Waco, a town that was once so wild it was nicknamed "Six-Shooter Junction." We think those herd-pushing cowboys might have liked a cooling cocktail like this one, which combines a favorite liquor from the South with juicy Texas oranges.

6	SPRIGS MINT
1	TEASPOON SUGAR
3	OUNCES SOUTHERN COMFORT
8	OUNCES CLUB SODA
	JUICE OF 1/2 ORANGE
	ICE
	ORANGE PEEL THINLY SLICED, FOR GARNISH

Using a spoon, crush the mint and sugar together in the bottom of highball glasses. Into each glass add equal parts Southern Comfort, soda, juice, and a few ice cubes. Stir, then garnish with orange slices.

Will Rogers Cooler

Makes 2 servings

Will, as you know, never met a man he didn't like. Well, we've never met a cowboy hat–wearing bartender we didn't like, and this drink came from one we think is tops. The name just seemed to fit.

ICE

3   OUNCES GIN

2   TABLESPOONS ORANGE JUICE, FRESHLY SQUEEZED

1   OUNCE DRY VERMOUTH

DASH OF TRIPLE SEC, ABOUT 10 DROPS

ORANGE PEEL THINLY SLICED, FOR GARNISH

Fill a cocktail shaker half full of ice cubes. Pour in the gin, orange juice, vermouth, and Triple Sec. Cover and shake well. Strain the drink into chilled cocktail glasses and serve. Garnish with an orange peel.

CHISHOLM TRAIL BIT

Most cowboys trailing cattle to Kansas cow towns were from Texas, but those from other places also were called "Texans." A traveler of the day described them this way: "In appearance a species of centaur, half horse, half man, with immense rattling spurs, tanned skin, and dare-devil, almost ferocious faces."

Trail Driving Days, *1952*

10

CHUCK-WAGON SECRETS

Glossary

Here's what you need to know about all the goodies that go into our *Texas Cowboy Kitchen* eats. None of this is rocket science, of course. Remember, it's all about making food that makes you feel tall in the saddle, and having fun on the trail in the process.

1015 ONION Developed at Texas A&M University, the state vegetable of Texas (so designated by the Legislature) is named for its ideal planting date, October 15. Available to consumers in the spring, this giant, white onion is noted for its sweetness.

ANCHO A broad, dried chile, it measures about 3 to 4 inches in length and is a dark reddish-brown. Flavor can range from mellow to strong, and the aroma is deep and slightly fruitlike. Anchos are made from fresh, green poblano chiles.

ASIAGO A full, nutty flavor is found in this semi-firm cheese from Italy made from cow's milk. Find it in small wheels.

BRAISE This cooking method is used to brown meat or vegetables in fat, such as oil, before cooking in a covered dish with a little liquid over low heat for an extended period.

BRINE, BRINING An intense solution of water, salt, and sugar is used with poultry for long-soaking to retain the meat's natural juices.

CABRITO The meat of a baby goat, which is typically roasted and very tender.

CACIOTTA A soft, Italian cow's-milk cheese perfect for melting inside enchiladas. Monterey jack can be substituted.

CAJETA A lush, rich brown syrup made from goat's milk and caramelized sugar.

CHAYOTE Popular with the Aztec and Mayan cultures, this light green fruit looks like a large, rutted pear but is actually prepared like a summer or acorn squash. Its mild flavor often calls for plenty of seasoning.

CHEVRE A French term for "goat cheese."

CHICKEN-FRIED A cooking technique in which a meat or vegetable is battered and deep-fried.

CHICKEN-FRIED STEAK Tenderized meat (such as sirloin, rib eye, or venison) dipped in a batter, floured, and deep-fried.

CHILE Often referred to as a pepper, chile pepper, or hot pepper, this pod is found throughout cuisines in the Americas, Asia, Africa, and even Europe. More than 200 varieties are thought to exist, and more than 100 are indigenous to Mexico. Found in sizes from less than 1 inch to more than 12 inches in length, chiles can be fresh or dried. Flavors range from extremely mild to exceptionally spicy.

CHILE RELLENO A Mexican specialty in which a fresh, green chile is stuffed with meat, cheese, or both. In some recipes, the chile is dipped in an egg batter and baked or fried.

PREVIOUS SPREAD
Odd Jobs in Camp [Joe Gleen, Stray Man for Sulphur Cattle Company, Gleeson, Arizona, and D. W. McFarland, Stray Man for the Wagon Rod Outfit, Making a Cinch; under the Wagon Reading is J. W. Haverty of Fort Huachuca], OR Range, Arizona. 1909.

TEXAS COWBOY KITCHEN BITE

For a great salsa, pico de gallo, onion jam, and onion rings, you absolutely must use a wonderfully sweet onion. While folks on the West Coast are addicted to Maui onions and everyone in the South loves those good Vidalia onions, we're blessed in Texas to have easy access to the incomparable 1015 onion. Acclaimed as the sweetest, mildest-tasting onions anywhere, the 1015s are grown in South Texas' Rio Grande Valley and go by the trade name of 1015 SuperSweet Onions. Generally available throughout the nation in grocery stores from mid-April through May, they're recognized for their Texas-sized magnitude and thin, dry skin. Cultivated to contain only scant amounts of the tear-inducing chemical called pyruvate, the 1015 is named for October 15, its ideal planting date.

TEXAS COWBOY KITCHEN BITE

There was no written record of chiles before Columbus came upon them in the New World in 1492. Today, the chile is the source for one of the most commonly used spices in the world. Food experts believe the chile originated in South America, but today there are hundreds of varieties grown in Mexico, New Mexico, and Texas.

Our food is certainly better for it. We use green chiles in many of our everyday foods, roasting it to add to macaroni and cheese or grits, or chopping it fresh to use on top of Frito pie. Good chiles to keep on hand include serranos, jalapeños, and habaneros, which are usually chopped fresh and make good additions to pico de gallo. Watch out for the intense heat of habaneros, however. Good roasting chiles are the mild varieties, such as New Mexico greens, which closely resemble Anaheims, and poblanos, which are stuffed for delicious chiles rellenos.

CHIPOTLE A dried jalapeño chile. A smoky flavor is characteristic.

CHORIZO Spicy, Mexican sausage.

CILANTRO Also called coriander, this leafy herb can resemble curly parsley or flat-leaf parsley but has a much more tart, intense flavor.

CORIANDER Refers to both the herb plant (see "cilantro") and seeds. Seeds are yellowish-tan, mildly fragrant, and have a flavor that seems to blend lemon, sage, and caraway. Whole seeds are used in pickling, and ground seed is used in baking and in cooking stews and soups.

CRAWFISH Also known as crayfish, the freshwater crustaceans look like tiny lobsters. Measuring about 3 to 6 inches in length, most come from Louisiana and Mississippi. The sweet, juicy meat goes in stews, salads, and tamales. Nicknames include crawdads and mudbugs.

CRÈME FRAÎCHE Matured, thickened cream has a tangy taste and lush, velvety texture.

CUMIN An ancient spice also called comino or cumino, the seed resembles a caraway and has a deep, peppery, almost smoky aroma and taste. Ground cumin is common in Mexican, Middle Eastern, and Asian cooking.

DEVIL Adding hot or spicy seasonings to a food creates a deviled dish.

DRIPPINGS Melted fat or juices that drip to the bottom of a pan in which meat is cooked. Drippings make a great base for gravy or sauce and can be added to flavor foods.

DRY-AGED BEEF Cuts of beef are hung in a humidity-controlled, cool space that is kept at 32° to 34°F for a period of 15 to 36 days.

DUTCH OVEN A large pot or kettle, typically made from cast iron, with a tight-fitting lid. Good for braising, stewing, and cooking over a fire, the ware is said to date to the Pennsylvania Dutch heritage of the 1700s.

FENNEL Aromatic plant resembling celery and often used in salads, stews, and soups. The aromatic, sweet flavor is slightly reminiscent of anise, but much more delicate.

GOAT CHEESE Made from goat's milk, the texture can range from creamy to crumbly. A tart flavor is characteristic.

GRITS Coarsely ground hominy that is cooked with milk or water.

HANGER STEAK Also called the hanging tender and the butcher's steak, this cut of beef originated as the French onglet. Technically, it is two small muscles connected by an elastic membrane that holds the cow's diaphragm. Beautifully succulent, it is best when cooked no more than medium rare.

HOMINY GRITS See "grits."

JAPANESE MANDOLINE A hand-operated machine with various, extremely sharp blades used for cutting vegetables into very thin slices, as well as to julienne vegetables. Equipped with a folding apparatus, mandolines come in wooden, heavy plastic, or stainless-steel construction.

KOSHER SALT Coarse-grained, additive-free salt with superior texture and flavor.

MASA HARINA Dough flour made from corn kernels that have been dried by the sun or fire and cooked in lime water, soaked, and ground. Used to make tamales.

OILS Peanut is preferable for frying because its durability tolerates high heat but resists easy burning. Olive is best for salad dressings and dips. Vegetable oil is good for marinating and for providing a wet base on meats that call for the use of dry rubs and seasoning blends.

PILONCILLA Mexican brown sugar, found in solid, cone shapes.

POBLANO Dark green, supple chile best used for stuffing in chile relleno recipes. The dried form is the ancho chile.

PORK BUTT Also called the pork shoulder butt, this boneless or bone-in cut of pork is perfect for long, slow, moist-heat cooking for flavorful tenderness.

PORTERHOUSE Cut from the large end of the short loin, this cut has a T-shaped bone and is suitable for grilling, broiling, and pan-cooking.

REMOULADE A classic French sauce that is served chilled with cold meat and fish. Made with homemade mayonnaise, mustard, herbs, and other additions.

RIB EYE Cut of beef from the choice area of the eye of the rib, this steak typically has the best flavor and texture due to marbling. Good for grilling, broiling, and pan-cooking.

RUBS A dry rub consists of seasonings and fresh or dried herbs. Wet rubs can contain seasonings, herbs, vegetable oil, minced fresh garlic, mustard, or other liquids.

SAFFRON The dried, pungent, aromatic spice that comes from the gold-orange stigma from a small purple crocus. Known as the most expensive spice in the world, it is sold in small quantities in powdered and thread form.

SAGE Mediterranean herb with narrow, oval, grayish-green leaves and an earthy-mint taste.

SERRANO A smallish, narrow, bright green chile.

SHORT RIBS Cut from the chuck, these rectangles of beef are about 2 inches wide and 3 inches long and contain layers of meat and fat, along with pieces of rib bone. Long, slow, moist-heat cooking makes these tender.

SOURDOUGH Slightly sour, tangy bread that gets its flavor from a special, carefully cultivated yeast starter.

TENDERLOIN From the center of the sirloin area, a long wedge is cut to produce particularly desirable steaks, such as filet mignon and medallions.

TOMATILLOS Sometimes called a Mexican green tomato, this smallish fruit bears a thin covering that feels like parchment paper. The meat is tart and is used in salsas, sauces, and stews.

TOSTADA A crisp-fried corn or flour tortilla used to make a crackerlike base for salads or layered dishes of meats, beans, and vegetables.

Sources and Resources

Here are some places that you can find ingredients for our *Texas Cowboy Kitchen* recipes. You'll also see sources here for more information on the Chisholm Trail and Texas cowboy heritage.

SPICE PURVEYORS

Pendery's World of Spices & Chiles
1407 Eighth Avenue
Fort Worth, TX 76104
(817) 924-3434
(800) 533-1870
www.penderys.com

P. Z.'s Bean and Spice Company
9806 Hillcroft
Houston, TX 77096
(713) 723-7001

**ONLINE SUPPLIERS
AND COOKING SITES**

CHEF'S
www.chefscatalog.com

Cooking.com
www.cooking.com

mexgrocer.com
www.mexgrocer.com

Lodge Cast Iron
www.lodgemfg.com

Tienda.com
www.tienda.com

MEAT PURVEYORS AND INFORMATION

Nolan Ryan's All-Natural Tender Aged Beef
P.O. Box 448
Huntsville, TX 77342-0448
(936) 436-1651
(877) 99-NOLAN
www.nolanryanbeef.com

Broken Arrow Ranch
P.O. Box 530,
104 Hwy. 27 West
Ingram, TX 78025
(830) 367-5875
(800) 962-4263
www.brokenarrowranch.com

Diamond H Ranch
5322 Hwy. 16 N.
Bandera, TX 78003
(830) 460-8406
www.texasgourmetquail.com

National Cattlemen's Beef Association
9110 E. Nichols Avenue #300
Centennial, CO 80112
(303) 694-0305
www.beef.org

Texas Beef Council
8708 Ranch Road 620 North
Austin, TX 78726
(512) 335-2333
www.txbeef.org

OTHER TEXAS FOODS AND PRODUCTS

Texas Department of Agriculture
Go Texan Program
Main Office:
1700 North Congress Avenue
Stephen F. Austin Building, 9th Floor
Austin, TX 78701
(877) 99-GOTEX
www.gotexan.org

Texas Wine & Grape
Growers Association
701 S. Main Street
Grapevine, TX 76051
(817) 424-0570
www.txwines.org

Jake Rains and His Pet Horse Comanche, Who Likes Chunks of Sourdough, Spur Ranch, Texas. ca. 1910.

Buck Reams Music and
Chuckwagon Cooking
P.O. Box 64171
Fort Worth, TX 76164
(817) 558-6656
www.BuckReams.com

**WESTERN ART AND
HISTORY MUSEUMS**
Amon Carter Museum
3501 Camp Bowie Boulevard
Fort Worth, TX 76107
(817) 738-1933
www.cartermuseum.org

Cattle Raisers Museum
1301 W. Seventh Street
Fort Worth, TX 76102
(817) 332-8551, (800) 242-7280
www.cattleraisersmuseum.org

Chisholm Trail Museum
1000 N. 29th Street
Duncan, OK 73534
(580) 252-6692
www.onthechisholmtrail.com

National Cowgirl Museum
and Hall of Fame
1720 Gendy Street
Fort Worth, TX 76107
(817) 336-4475
www.cowgirl.net

*Bronc Rider for the Bar Diamond
Bar Riding a Sunfisher [outside
Bonham, Texas]. 1906–1907.*

Texas Cowboy Hall of Fame
128 E. Exchange Avenue
Fort Worth, TX 76106
(817) 626-7131
www.texascowboyhalloffame.com

Stockyards Museum
131 E. Exchange Avenue
Fort Worth, TX 76106
(817) 625-5087

Sid Richardson Collection
of Western Art
309 Main Street
Fort Worth, TX 76102
(817) 332-6554, (888) 332-6554
www.sidrichardsonmuseum.org

**GENERAL FORT WORTH
AND TEXAS INFORMATION**
Fort Worth Convention
& Visitors Bureau
415 Throckmorton Street
Fort Worth, TX 76102
(817) 336-8791, (800) 433-5747
www.fortworth.com

Texas Historical Commission
1511 Colorado
Austin, TX 78701
(512) 463-6100
www.thc.state.tx.us
(Request a Chisholm Trail Map)

AMON CARTER MUSEUM COLLECTION
All the historical photographs are
reproduced from the original negatives
in the Erwin E. Smith Collection of
the Library of Congress on deposit
at the Amon Carter Museum, Fort
Worth, Texas.
www.cartermuseum.org.

**CENTER FOR AMERICAN
HISTORY, UT-AUSTIN**
Historical map shown on endpapers
and page 11 courtesy of the Center
for American History, UT-Austin.
Jack Potter's Map of Cattle Trails,
1935. Prepared by A. C. Loveless,
Clayton, New Mexico.

Index

Thanks, Y'all

AS IS THE CASE with most cookbooks, this one was a labor of love for food, cooking, and heritage. None of it would have been possible without the unfailing enthusiasm of friends, family, and colleagues.

First, our friends at Texas Monthly Custom Publishing pulled us through daunting days and sleepless nights of planning, writing, rewriting, and editing. From the moment we first discussed the idea of a book celebrating Texas food and history of the Chisholm Trail, Cathy Casey, Sara McCabe, and Missy Colbert climbed right in the wagon with us and never doubted their wisdom (or ours). Sara made the deal happen, and Missy spent countless months dispensing guidance, encouragement, and well-timed humor. We'll never be able to repay that debt.

Through them, we had the unbelievable good fortune to work with extraordinary designers DJ Stout and Julie Savasky. Their vision and passion for our dream shines on every page of this brilliantly designed book. Through TMCP we also gained the keen eye and sharp wit of editor Brian Sweany and researching smarts of Valerie Wright.

We were also blessed with the front-line editing of the very insightful and endlessly supportive Catherine Madigan. And when it came to food photography, we had to look no farther than the genius of our close friends, photographer Ralph Lauer and stylist Meda Kessler, who worked with an impossible deadline and even spent Christmas Day cooking and shooting beautiful food to make us look good.

We owe a wealth of thanks to Gwin Grogan Grimes for her valuable recipe-testing and practical advice.

A large debt of gratitude goes to our agent, Lisa Ekus; our editor, Jean Lucas; and our many colleagues at Andrews McMeel.

Several Fort Worth retailers provided wonderful materials and props used in Ralph and Meda's photos. They are Leigh-Boyd Antiques, Domain XCIV Antiques, Pier 1 Imports, and the Montgomery Street Antique Mall.

Also on the homefront, we had the good fortune to work with Barbara McCandless, Ron Tyler, Jeff Guy, Pam Graham, and Callie Morfeld Vincent at the esteemed Amon Carter Museum. The inclusion of extraordinary photographs by Erwin E. Smith was a greater gift than we could have possibly imagined.

Over the three years that we planned and produced this book, a cast of wonderful characters helped, prodded, and cheered us on. They include Doug Harmon at the Fort Worth Convention & Visitors Bureau, Patricia Sharpe at *Texas Monthly*, and Fort Worth photographer Rhonda Hole; chefs, food experts, and cookbook authors such as Kristine Ackerman and Stephan Pyles; and the chefs and cooks in Chapter 3, who loaned us recipes. Friends who came through with expertise and guidance at exactly the right moments include Dennis Hayes and Barbara Rodriguez.

And every step of the way, our families and closest friends kept us going. Those whose faith, support, and friendship went beyond reasonable expectations include countless members of our large families.

We are also appreciative to Nolan Ryan for his support and for the wealth of information from the Texas Historical Commission, the Cattle Ranchers Association, and the various Chisholm Trail historical centers throughout Texas. And for all American cattle ranchers, as well as Buck Reams and his fellow chuck-wagon cooks and Red Steagall and other gifted cowboy poets, this is for you. Lovers of Texas history, culture, and lore are blessed by your existence.